"A moving story . . . A portrait of a unique love that beautifully evokes pictures from the past."

—*De Telegraaf*

"Van der Zijl tells a compelling story and knows how to develop the characters in this love story using the social and historical background of their lives . . . A beautiful book."

—Hans Renders in *Het Parool*

"A beautiful portrait . . . Her story moved me to tears."

—*HP/De Tijd*

THE
BOY
BETWEEN
WORLDS

OTHER TITLES BY
ANNEJET VAN DER ZIJL

An American Princess

ANNEJET VAN DER ZIJL

Bestselling author of *An American Princess*

THE
BOY
BETWEEN
WORLDS

A BIOGRAPHY

TRANSLATED BY KRISTEN GEHRMAN

Text copyright © 2004, 2009 by Annejet van der Zijl

Translation copyright © 2019 by Kristen Gehrman

Previously published as *Sonny Boy* by Nijgh & Van Ditmar and Em. Querido's Uitgeverij in the Netherlands in 2004 and 2009. Translated from Dutch by Kristen Gehrman. First published in English by AmazonCrossing in 2019.

Published by AmazonCrossing, Seattle
www.apub.com

Amazon, the Amazon logo, and AmazonCrossing are trademarks of Amazon.com, Inc., or its affiliates.

ISBN-13: 9781542007313 (hardcover)
ISBN-10: 1542007313 (hardcover)
ISBN-13: 9781542040099 (paperback)
ISBN-10: 1542040094 (paperback)

Cover design by Shasti O'Leary Soudant

Unless otherwise noted, all photos are courtesy of a private collection.

Printed in the United States of America
First edition

For my sister, Sietske van der Zijl

When there are grey skies
I don't mind the grey skies
You make them blue, Sonny Boy

Friends may forsake me
Let them all forsake me
I still have you, Sonny Boy

You came from heaven
And I know your worth
You've made a heaven
For me right here on earth

And the angels, they grew lonely
Took you because they were lonely
Now I'm lonely too, Sonny Boy[1]

"Sonny Boy" from the film *The Singing Fool*,
sung by Al Jolson, 1928

Official, academic history has, as I said, nothing to tell us about the differences in intensity of historical occurrences. To learn about that, you must read biographies, not those of statesmen but the all-too-rare ones of unknown individuals.[2]

Sebastian Haffner, *Defying Hitler: A Memoir*

THE RIVER, 1923

Waldemar was a swimmer. At not yet fifteen, he could already swim the twelve and a half miles from Domburg, past the forgotten plantations and busy loading docks, all the way to his mother's large house on the Waterfront. This was the marathon route, reserved for the very best swimmers in Paramaribo—and the smartest ones at that, for the Suriname River was like a crocodile with one eye open: calm, but deadly. On his way to school in the morning, the water sloshed languidly against the banks as the river flowed to the sea. But by the time Waldemar came home in the afternoon, the water level had dropped by several meters; the river's muddy bowels were left glistening in the sun, and the Sabaku herons would be searching for food among the stranded boats. And when night fell, it was as though the river had suddenly been pulled upstream by a mighty invisible force, and its waves would lick the trunks of the almond trees growing along the Waterfront.

The river played just as mysterious a game with the wind. Sometimes she'd obediently conform to the wind's wishes, other times she would stubbornly fight against it, her waters rippling and churning, stewing from all sides. A stealthy killer, that's what she was. And there wasn't a family in Suriname who didn't have an overly confident son or nephew who had been swallowed up by Paramaribo's lifeline. Still, they kept diving in, the boys with their slender brown bodies, shooting through the water like fish. Because conquering the river was like conquering the world—it brought respect in the eyes of classmates and furtive glances from the giggly groups of girls in pristine white dresses who hung out in the main square on Sundays.

Waldemar was known as a quiet boy, sometimes even aloof. He wasn't a daredevil like his older brother, nor was he spoiled royalty like his little sister, who was all too happy to flaunt her position as the daughter of one of the richest men in the colony. But when he swam, something extraordinary happened. Even the biggest talkers on the docks would fall quiet, and everyone's eyes would become fixated on the wondrous whirl of boy and water. It was as if he and the river were playing together.

Waldemar was never scared of the hungry river, for he knew her like no one else. When he was just a little boy, he would study her from the veranda and be lulled to sleep by the sound of her waves. And as he grew older, he discovered how she was constantly pulled back and forth by the moon and ocean, and how, even when the wind raged against her, she stubbornly tried to carry out her tides. He knew the movements of the water like the rituals of his mother's household. Swimming, he'd learned, wasn't only a matter of muscles. It was about respecting the river, taking advantage of her whims and fancies, knowing where to swim and, above all, when.

Once every four weeks, a steamboat from the Royal West-Indian Mail Service left for Holland. The flags on the festively decorated ship flapped in the wind, and a farewell cannon was fired from Fort Zeelandia. The passengers on deck craned their necks to catch one last glimpse of their loved ones down below. Waldemar and his friends would hop in a little boat and follow in the ship's frothy wake for miles, all the way to Fort New Amsterdam, where the Suriname River swirled into the equally mighty Commewijne, and one could just make out the blue of the ocean. After shouting a final farewell to the passengers, the boys would untie the ropes and paddle back to the city. But not

Waldemar. He would dive into the brackish water and swim home. Stroke by stroke, yard by yard, he'd find his rhythm and effortlessly cleave through the water. He swam, cleansed by the current, until there was nothing left but himself, son of Suriname, raised by the river. She carried him. The water was his friend.

1

November in Holland

Nowhere on earth can be so wet and dreary, the countryside so sodden and desolate, the streets so deserted in the pouring rain, as Holland in late autumn. And never is a big city so comforting—its steamed-up café windows offering endless promises of warmth and shelter before the winter sets in. It's the time of year when love can sneak in on stocking feet and creep into the hearts of the very people who feel old and tired, whose hope for better days is threatening to collapse under the weight of the past.

Rika Hagenaar-van der Lans had a hundred reasons to be tired in the autumn of 1928. She was tired of endlessly bickering with her husband, who refused to accept that she had left him for good and assumed she was going to come crawling back to him with her tail between her legs. She was tired of her fruitless attempts to build an independent life as a woman with four young children and no profession or means of survival. She was tired of her family, who had taken her in, but who had made it abundantly clear that a union before God shall never be broken, and certainly not by someone who—and this was the real crux—had made her own bed and now so vehemently refused to lie in it.

As if Rika could ever forget how, as a young woman, she had done everything in her power to be able to marry, "till death do us part," the man who had now become the antithesis of her dreams. At the time it had all seemed like a romantic fairy tale, a sort of *Romeo and Juliet*, but set in a conventional middle-class suburb of The Hague around the turn of the twentieth century. Hendrika Wilhelmina Johanna, or Rika for short, was born on September 29, 1891, the oldest daughter of Catholic potato merchant Jans van der Lans. Her mother had descended from a family of ill repute, which might have been why she was so Victorian in her views—tough on oneself, tough on others. "She was like the strong woman from Scripture," as her prayer card would later read.[3] She ruled over her five daughters and three sons with an iron fist, fully backed by God and the Roman Catholic Church, while her husband devoted himself to his business and, with visible satisfaction, assumed the role of an indulgent paterfamilias.

The Van der Lans daughters were a striking lot: beautiful girls with a strong presence, constantly quarreling and trying to outdo each other, but at the same time inseparable. Rika was the eldest and therefore predestined to become her mother's faithful assistant, but she wasn't cut out for the role. She was too much like the heroines from the books all the girls were reading in those days: too sensitive and emotional for the stringent, noisy environment she'd been raised in, but also too inclined toward the kind of independent thinking that was considered far from suitable for a young girl of her time. There was a certain sense of restlessness about her, and her striking, nearly black eyes were constantly searching for something more than the everyday monotony.

As a young girl, Rika was devoutly religious. She grew up in a time when the church and parents conspired to make children profoundly aware of how indebted they were to those who had raised them, and year after year, children diligently scribbled the same sappy texts their dear priest found so endearing. In commemoration of her first holy communion, in 1903, Rika wrote a thank-you letter to her parents on angel-decorated stationery:

> How could I ever repay all that He has done for me
> and continues to do for me today? The entire debt
> I shall never be able to pay, but I will do everything
> in my power. This morning I prayed to Jesus to pour
> out his divine blessings upon you. Believe me, my
> Dear Parents, never shall I forget you in my prayers.
> I will stay true to God and continue on the path of
> righteousness.[4]

In the photo taken to celebrate the occasion, twelve-year-old Rika looks like a true bride of Christ. Nothing in her eyes would lead one to suspect that she'd ever long for anything other than the "divine pleasure" of Christ[5] that she—in her own words—learned to taste that day. Four years later, she looked at Willem Hagenaar through the same eyes, with the same earnest devotion, and there was no indication that she'd ever long for anything other than him.

***

Willem was nineteen when he first laid eyes on the oldest Van der Lans daughter. With her delicate face and plump arms, she looked like she'd stepped right off a postcard; it was love at first sight. He was a tall student with an intense gaze, the very image of the kind of man Rika had dreamed of marrying. Their love held little promise for the future, however, because Willem's father was a Protestant headmaster with an intense aversion to all things papal. On top of that, he considered the Van der Lans family ordinary middle-class folk at best. Rika's parents were equally horrified by the thought of their daughter marrying outside of her faith. In their eyes, marrying a Protestant would plunge her into a state of irrevocable mortal sin.

When it came out that, despite it being strictly forbidden, the young couple was continuing to meet in secret, Rika's mother took drastic measures. At the age of seventeen, Rika was sent to Sacré Coeur, the Catholic boarding school in Moerdijk on the other side of the Hollands Diep river, a good thirty-seven miles from The Hague. Her solution seemed to work. Rika's letters home were well mannered and pious, with no mention of the young Hagenaar. Meanwhile, however, the forced separation did nothing but fuel the clandestine love affair. Determined, Willem endured one technical exam after the other in pursuit of his childhood dream: a job at the Rijkswaterstaat, the state agency for water infrastructure and a very fashionable place to work at the time. As the organization responsible for the country's roads, bridges, canals, and dikes, the Rijkswaterstaat was a driving force behind industrialization, which was essential for Dutch well-being, especially now that the kingdom's colonial sources of income were drying up.

In 1911, Willem passed the Rijkswaterstaat's entrance exam. The first thing he did was jump on his bike and pedal all the way to Moerdijk at breakneck speed. When he got there, he climbed over the high wall separating the school from the sunny outside world, pushed his way through the shrieking girls and shocked nuns until he found Rika, and took her with him. The young couple turned up in The Hague the next day. Rika had officially run off with her lover for the night, and in doing so, given up her honor forever. On both sides, there was little the parents could do but consent to their marriage.

In their wedding portrait, Willem looks decidedly triumphant, while his bride stares dreamily into the camera with her gazellelike eyes, lost in the ultimate romance of the moment. True love had prevailed, just like in her books and the silent movies she had seen at the cinema. But no matter how dreamy she looked, Rika was no pushover. Given that her parents had refused to attend the ceremony and forbidden her brothers and sisters to attend as well, Rika and Willem rode by her parents' house in the wedding carriage after the ceremony so they could at least see how beautiful the black sheep of the family looked in her virginal white wedding gown. This only added to Mrs. Van der Lans's outrage.

The young couple moved into a villa that belonged to the Rijkswaterstaat in Apeldoorn, a small city in the Veluwe forest that, since the introduction of a canal, had developed into the center of the national paper industry. It was here that Rika gave birth to her first son, in 1915, who was named after his father. Two years later came a daughter who, as a peace offering toward the family in The Hague, was named after Rika's mother, Lambertina. The tension between Rika and her family had abated, mainly because the Van der Lanses had enough Roman Catholic pragmatism in their hearts to realize that a lifelong excommunication of their favorite daughter wouldn't do anyone any good. So, they lit an extra candle for her soul on Sundays and took tremendous pleasure in their first grandchildren, who—much to the Van der Lanses' delight and the Hagenaars' chagrin—were being raised Catholic.

It was an era of optimism. The factories were churning, the chimneys were smoking, and daily life was being transformed by one exciting invention after the other—from electricity to automobiles to radios and portable gramophones. Shortly after little Bertha was born, Willem was transferred to Den Bosch. The Den Bosch branch of the Rijkswaterstaat was known for being exceptionally social, and the young Hagenaar couple was welcomed into the circle with open arms. They were an attractive duo and seemed to be a perfect match for each other. Both exceedingly charming, both vain, and both lovers of fine clothing, going out, and dancing, they seemed to fall ever more passionately in love—like two "turtledoves," as Rika's sisters teased.

Rika and Willem took to the rich Roman Catholic life in the Brabant capital like fish to water, and in 1921, their third child was born. The little boy was named Jan after his maternal grandfather and perhaps also after the impressive Saint John's Cathedral near their home. One year later, Willem commissioned an official family portrait. He was a successful man in the prime of his life with three beautiful children and a wife whose mischievous look was enough to make any man envy him. It seemed as if nothing or no one could ever stand in the way of their happiness.

***

As they say, the Lord giveth and the Lord taketh away, and the Rijkswaterstaat was no exception. The agency took excellent care of its employees, but its head office decided what they did and where they lived. And in the fall of 1924, the agency decided to move Willem Hagenaar up a rung on the career ladder. He was promoted to the position of dike warden of Goeree-Overflakkee, an island in South Holland that, for the entirety of its existence, had been dependent on a complicated system of seawalls, dunes, and dikes to keep out the capricious North Sea. Thus, the Rijkswaterstaat envoy was an important man, even more important than the local mayor. In December, shortly after the birth of their fourth child, Henk—or the "carnival baby," as he was lovingly called because he must have been conceived during the festival season—the Hagenaar family moved to Goeree.

The bare, windswept island couldn't have been more different from elegant Den Bosch. Although it wasn't very far from the major cities in the western Netherlands, Goeree was still extremely isolated. The only contact with the outside world was via a ferry that traveled between Middelharnis and Hellevoetsluis once a day. Goedereede was a small town behind the dike with a few shabby shops and nothing of the luxury that Rika had grown accustomed to in Brabant. The islanders were conservative through and through and so devoutly religious that they went to church twice on Sunday. They regarded the modern trends that were gaining steam in the big cities with tremendous suspicion. It seemed as if time had come to a halt, and it wouldn't be starting up again anytime soon.

Born and raised in the city, Rika knew very little about rural life—only that it had always seemed so idyllic on her springtime day trips to the countryside. But during her first winter in her new town, she must have discovered that all those blossoming flowers and frolicking lambs were just a rosy picture of the slow, hard reality of farm life. She felt as if she'd been buried alive on the island and grew restless with the steady rhythm of nature. She preferred to buy her flowers neatly wrapped in paper from a stand rather than to watch them slowly sprout in the black soil of her own backyard. She longed for the bustle of the city and the sense of freedom it offered. More than anything, she missed the anonymity. Everywhere she went in the small town, all eyes were on her. The locals eyed the new mistress of the Rijkswaterstaat house with a mixture of curiosity and mistrust. She was Catholic, and thus a heathen by default, and you could see it in her eyes—the sin lying in wait.

Rika's attempts to make peace with her new life only made things worse. She went swimming in the sea near Ouddorp, which was, in the stern eyes of her fellow villagers, a highly unsuitable activity for a married woman. Her spacious kitchen was always full of children—her own, their little friends from the village, and their cousins from the city—and Rika was prone to organizing all kinds of gatherings, including a "heathen" party for carnival. And one day she set up Willem's big portable gramophone in the empty salon and started hosting the kind of parties they'd been used to in Den Bosch. The children bore a hole in their bedroom floor so they could spy on the fun below. The whole island talked about Rika's scandalous soirees: wild dance parties until late in the night—clearly the work of the devil himself.

It didn't take long for the stories of Rika's unseemly behavior to reach Willem. He, for one, was quite happy in their new town. He enjoyed his status and the respect he received as Mr. Hagenaar from The Hague. He was also much less bothered by the conservative attitudes on the island. Most likely, he was more comfortable with their straight-and-narrow norms and values—the same ones he'd grown up with himself—than he had been with the Catholic gaiety in Den Bosch. Willem loved Rika with a burning, even obsessive, passion, and he had always had trouble with the fact that other men found her attractive. This had inspired numerous bouts of jealousy, though always unwarranted. He could hardly forbid her from laughing and moving about freely as she did. But now, he finally had a reason to demand a bit of restraint. A man of his position, he reasoned, simply couldn't be yoked with a wife who made herself the subject of gossip. The least she could do was try to conform to his role on the island. After all, his job provided them with the beautiful roof over their heads, two household servants, and a thick layer of butter on their daily bread.

But no matter how good-humored and easygoing Rika was in daily life, she wasn't one to be forced into anything, as her parents had already figured out at their own expense. She found the weekly sermons in the local church—about how wives were to submit to their husbands—downright absurd. Perhaps that was how things worked in the Hagenaar home, but when she was growing up, her mother had been in charge of everyone, especially her father. Rather than succumbing to this new way of life, she only became more disturbed by it, and all the things about Willem she'd once been so attracted to—his power, his sense of purpose, his passion—started weighing on her as heavily as life on the island itself. Rika's restlessness aroused panic in Willem. The less control he had over her, the more threatened he felt, and the more jealous and irascible he became. And the harder he tried to rein his unruly wife, the harder she tried to break free.

With the same passion they'd loved each other with in their early years, they fought with each other now. Sometimes they took after Willem's parents and stewed for days in silence. Other times they exploded, making a loud scene as Rika's parents were wont to do. However, by this point in their marriage, Willem and Rika were no longer capable of passionate reconciliation. When they fought, their oldest son, Wim, would carry glasses of water back and forth between his parents in a desperate attempt to calm the storm. Even eight-year-old Bertha's friends started to notice that the atmosphere at her house had become very tense.

In the spring of 1926, a year and a half after they'd moved to Goeree, the Hagenaars posed for another family portrait, this time in the grass under the blossoming fruit trees behind their house. As idyllic as the setting was, their faces tell another story. In the photo, Willem has a markedly wry smile on his face, and Rika looks far from happy. Though she had always had a voluptuous figure, she has clearly put on weight and even looks a bit dowdy. Her husband viewed the extra pounds as a reason to seek attention and affirmation from other women, many of whom had their eye on him. This created yet another source of conflict between the couple. Their marriage was quickly unraveling at the seams, and they kept the island's gossip mill turning day and night. Willem Hagenaar had neither his wife nor his temper under control, and it reached a point where, in his anger, he couldn't control his hands either.

***

At the end of February 1928, Rika fled to The Hague. She took only Henk, the toddler, with her. She left her three older children in the loving hands of their maid, Jans, a girl from the island who had proved herself exceptionally devoted to the Hagenaar family. Rika's parents, however, did not welcome their daughter with open arms. Marrying a Protestant had been bad enough, but no number of candles or prayers in the world could absolve her of a divorce. To them, the situation was clear: their oldest daughter was having another one of her overly emotional fits of passion, and she needed to come to terms with her husband—the sooner the better. Despite his being Protestant, they had always found him rather charming.

But there was no way Rika was going back to the island, and in the end, she was taken in by one of her sisters. Jo van der Lans knew from her own experience that there was no saving a doomed marriage. Her

German husband, whom she'd been set up with by her own father, had left her a few years earlier. Since then, she had supported herself and her two young daughters by renting rooms in The Hague's Bloemen- en Bomenbuurt, the "flowers and trees" neighborhood, which sounded much greener than it was. The royal capital of the Netherlands had long played host to soldiers on furlough from the colonies; therefore, there was a high demand for temporary rentals. For single, uneducated women, renting out rooms was one of the only ways to earn a decent living.

That spring, Rika did what women often do after making a major life decision: she chopped off her long, dark locks. Having rediscovered her old bravado, she sent a photo of herself with her short, modern bob to Goeree: "Mama at the beach!" the caption read. The rest of the children joined her in The Hague in June. "Jan reunited with his mother!" Rika wrote happily on a photo of them at the beach in Scheveningen, where she took the children almost every day in an effort to compensate for the major changes in their lives. For the oldest boys, in particular, the move was a disaster. Wim and Jan had spent wonderful years on the boundless island, where, as the children of the dike warden, they were free to roam around in the dunes—their father had even had two wooden playhouses built just for them. Now they found themselves cooped up in a stuffy upstairs apartment in a new housing district in the western part of The Hague, where the flowery street names were a sharp contrast to the tightly packed housing blocks. Rika's oldest sons were as unhappy here as their mother had been in Goeree, and they fervently hoped that their hot-tempered parents would make up soon.

Willem Hagenaar also assumed that his spouse would ultimately choose money over freedom and would humbly return to her stylish life as a Rijkswaterstaat wife. What else could she do? She couldn't count on any support from her parents, and her sister could barely provide for herself and her own children, let alone an entire extra family—and the only thing she had learned during her time at the boarding school in Moerdijk was how to be a lady. But Rika didn't go back. She decided she'd much rather follow Jo's example and become a landlady, even if it meant giving up her life of luxury to become a sort of servant—cooking, washing, and toiling away for strangers.

In October 1928, Rika found an upper-floor apartment on the Azaleastraat, not far from her sister's place. It was around that time that she received her first boarder. He was introduced to her by Christien, a cousin of Willem's with whom the boarder had been living at the time. Rika had always had a good relationship with Christien, if only for the fact that she, too, had ventured into a controversial marriage. For all the uproar Willem and Rika's relationship had caused at the time, it was nothing compared to the tumult that erupted when Christien came home in 1919 with the news that she was pregnant by a black man whom she planned to marry. Her fiancé-to-be was from Suriname and had just stepped off the boat a year earlier with nothing but a stuffed crocodile and a bow and arrow for luggage.

The Hagenaar family's idea of people of color consisted of ferocious tribesmen in straw skirts—with bones through their noses—dancing around steaming pots, like the people they'd seen in the educational films at the cinema. To their tremendous surprise, Christien's lover, David Millar, turned out to be neat as a pin, with stylish spectacles, tidy clothes, and manners that could win over many a Dutch heart. Moreover, he was a man of great ambition, and shortly after he arrived in Holland, he became friends with an egg dealer in The Hague, Albert Plesman, who was in the process of establishing the Koninklijke Luchtvaart Maatschappij. Six years later, Millar was the financial director of a rapidly growing airline known as KLM.

"Uncle Dave," as Rika's children called their father's exotic cousin, was enamored with anything that had to do with modern technology. As soon as he could afford it, he bought himself a motorcycle with a sidecar, which he promptly drove into the Haarlemmertrekvaart canal with his young family on board. Still, this didn't stop him from exploring the Netherlands on his motorcycle, and in the spring of 1927, he paid a visit to Goeree-Overflakkee. The island was up in arms—no one had ever seen a black man before, let alone one traveling alone on a roaring motorcycle. Who cared if the older people in the village were calling it a sign of the apocalypse—the Hagenaar family donned leather helmets and goggles and proudly posed for a portrait with their extraordinary "uncle" and his motorcycle. Rika, in particular, had really hit it off with the man from Suriname: his easygoing, lighthearted way of doing things, his taste for adventure, all the faraway places he'd been— his visit had been a breath of fresh air in the oppressive world of Goeree.

For Christien Hagenaar, however, the romance of her exotic marriage had long since worn off. Dutch through and through, Christien struggled to cope with the tropical ways of her husband and his fellow countrymen. She was not at all amused when David announced in the fall of 1927 that a relative of his would be arriving from Paramaribo. Officially, the boy was a nephew, but the two looked so much alike that it soon became clear that he was more like a half brother. This didn't surprise Christien in the least. As far as she could tell, the whole colony was an utterly primitive, degenerate mess. She couldn't stand the thought of having yet another black man in her respectable household, and she didn't mince words about wanting to be rid of their new guest—she was all too happy to have cousin Rika take him off her hands.

2

Waldemar's World

Waldemar Nods had known from a young age that one day he would be an ocean swimmer. This had nothing to do with his swimming abilities but everything to do with the fact that he belonged to an elite group of boys with parents who could afford to send them to study in Holland, that faraway wonderland on the other side of the ocean. He and his friends were the pride of Paramaribo, the best that Suriname had to offer, and upon their return, they would be ushered into highbrow positions where they would earn double the salary of someone who had been educated in the colony. All good things came from Holland; that's just the way it was. And it was no wonder—when you consider that Suriname had been so literally created by its colonizers that it could almost be called a Dutch product.

The only ones who had had any real claim to the Wild Coast of the Guianas, which was discovered around 1500 by Spanish navigators lusting after gold, were the shy native tribes roaming the area at the time. But they were skilled in covering their tracks, and when the Portuguese arrived, they vanished into the vast jungle without protest and without leaving a trace. Meanwhile, their home was tossed around by European powers in search of conquerable land and colonial riches. In the end, it was small but reckless Holland that—in exchange for what would later become New York—claimed the promising land around the Suriname River in 1667. By that time, the colony's bountiful lowlands were covered with flourishing plantations, and the settlement that the natives had named Parmobo, or "place of flowers," had expanded into one of the most handsome cities in South America: Paramaribo, also known as "the Pearl of the West." But as beautiful as the landscape was, it was a harsh and primitive place to live. In that era, the West Indian colonies were viewed as a kind of trash pit of Europe. Their thin layer of elite white society was made up of people the Old World had wanted to get rid of or who had their own reasons to leave: Jewish-Portuguese planters; French Huguenots; poor farmers; and a hodge-podge of dangerous and not-so-dangerous criminals, fortune seekers, and adventurers. The lower echelons of society were made up of black African laborers who, because they were seemingly able to withstand the merciless heat, were purchased by the thousands on the West African coast and trafficked to the colony by Dutch slave traders from Zeeland.

In the centuries that followed, the slaves were treated reasonably well in the colony—at least in most cases. This was largely due to the fact that the whites knew they were outnumbered, and they wanted to avoid any kind of uprising. Moreover, everyone who had been sent, lured, or forced to this sweltering land in the middle of nowhere was ultimately dependent on each other. When winds of change swept across the world at the end of the nineteenth century carrying ideas of liberty, equality, and fraternity, Holland, too, was forced to heed the cries for universal freedom. In 1863, it became one of the last nations in the world to abolish slavery. But it turned out that for some, the reality of freedom wasn't exactly the triumph that the abolitionists had envisioned from the comfort of their salons on the other side of the world. The white plantation owners cashed in on the damages they received from the Dutch government and returned to Europe, leaving the colony behind with no leadership or capital to keep up with the Industrial Revolution. As plantation life crumbled, so did Suriname's social structure. Centuries-old communities fell apart, entire demographic groups were left adrift, and many former slaves fell into a state of extreme poverty that would have been unthinkable under their old masters.

Then the land itself came to the emerging population's rescue. In 1876, a group of explorers discovered in the eastern part of the country along the Lawa River what the Spanish navigators had been so desperately searching for three centuries earlier: gold. Black men headed into the jungle in droves, and all of Suriname was struck with gold fever. Sleepy Paramaribo developed into a booming, bustling gold town. But although the Pearl of the West had taken on a golden sparkle and was by no means lacking in colonial grandeur, it never really had the romantic appeal of other cities in the Dutch West Indies. The shiny veneer of civilization had always been thin, and there was still something wild and untamable about the Surinamese capital. And even though slavery was a thing of the past, racial discrimination was not. Color still determined social status, and having whiter skin improved one's chances of a successful life.

***

The slower the pace, the less that happens, and the less that happens, the more people gossip. And Paramaribo was certainly no exception. The city was brimming with old coteries from the end of the nineteenth century, when ladies in high-society circles had little to do but fan themselves and count the days until the next opportunity to don a new dress. The marriage of Koos Nods and Eugenie Elder in 1904 had people talking for months. For he, despite all his money and sweet-talking, was nothing but a gold digger, a ruffian with tanned black skin, whereas she was a lady in every sense of the word: proper, well-bred, and above all, nearly white.

Waldemar's mother bore the name of a bona fide plantation owner, which in the colony was a status symbol in itself. The fact that her ancestor, William Elder, had been nothing but a simple drummer who had enlisted in the colonial army because he had absolutely no prospects in Scotland, didn't matter in the least. What mattered was that he had worked his way up to owning a small but prosperous coffee and cacao plantation and that he had given not only freedom, but also his own untarnished name to his black mistress and their children. Since then, for generation after generation, the Elder women had chosen their patrons very carefully, until eventually their bloodline was nearly white—*opgekleurd*, or "upcolored," as it was called. The fact that there had never been a wedding wasn't the least bit unusual in the colonial world. Nonwhite people simply didn't marry—it was even forbidden under slavery—and white men all the way up to the governor himself were known to openly have relationships with black women. As a disheartened priest once stated: "The white lily of chastity will not flourish in tropical lands."[6] The best a woman of color could hope for was a relatively stable concubinage, otherwise known as a "Surinamese marriage."

Eugenie and her younger sister, Marie, had been raised by their mother, Cornelia, and were fully aware of their special status and the opportunities their light skin afforded them. Their mother's greatest fear was "blackening" the bloodline; she considered any contact with the black men who had gotten off the plantation a bit later than she did something to be avoided at all costs. Women of color with any ambition would never be caught barefoot—a sure sign of bondage during slavery. They were careful to stay out of the sun so as not to darken their skin and behaved as prudishly as they believed the Dutch women themselves did.

Eugenie was a quiet, God-fearing girl. She taught Sunday school at the stately Lutheran church on the Waterfront. Since the abolition of slavery, this formerly white conservative bulwark had gradually grown into the lively gathering point of the *blaka bakra*, the "black whites," as the Creole elite who rubbed shoulders with the upper layers of white society were called. Like her mother and grandmother, Eugenie seemed predestined to become the concubine of a distinguished white man, although a legal marriage with a successful, light-skinned black person would technically have been possible in those enlightened times as well. Nevertheless, associating with a man of color was still as taboo as in the not-so-distant past, when "amorous congress" between a white woman and a black man was punishable by death.

It was thus a complete mystery to everyone how the proper Sunday school teacher could have ever gotten involved with a black man, and how Koos Nods ever convinced her to be his wife. Granted, the clock was ticking—Eugenie was over thirty, after all. And as the saying went, "money makes a person's skin lighter." If that were true, then Eugenie's fiancé was one white lily. The fact that Koos had struck gold wasn't really all that unusual. The Surinamese ground proved generous, and he wasn't the only hopeful gold miner—*gowtuman*—to hit the mother lode. But the fact that he had managed to hang on to his fortune and become one of the richest men in the colony was exceptional.

Most of the *porknokkers*—as the gold seekers were called because they lived on dried meat in the jungle—enjoyed what chronicler Jacques Samuels called a "short but glorious life."[7] They burned through their profits in no time, diligently helped by family, friends, and anyone who managed to associate with them. Just as in the time of slavery, Surinamese families were expected to share everything with each other. Yet for someone who grew up in such a collective society, Koos was quite noticeably a loner. Maybe it was in his blood. His mother, Mietje, was born on a remote cotton plantation on the Atlantic coast, where Carib tribes still roamed in the surrounding jungle. Mietje's mother was reportedly the product of an encounter between a field slave and one of those last indigenous inhabitants. Those final remaining tribes were described by a priest as follows:

Every Indian, albeit the Arawak to a lesser extent than
the Caribs, from the time of his youth, is raised to be a
completely independent person, recognizing no one as his
superior. This makes him self-conceited and egotistical.
He must be free—independent from everyone—his own
king.[8]

This description matched Jacobus Theodorus Gerardus Nods to a
T. Not only did he see absolutely no reason to squander his money on
his poor family and opportunistic friends, he also wasn't the least bit
troubled by any feelings of inferiority that many black men harbored as
a result of slavery. Born in 1872, he was a child of the first truly free generation of Suriname. Growing up, he had profited from the auspicious
work of missionaries, who had been scrupulously kept away from the
colonies during slavery for fear that they might introduce the slaves to
the idea that they, too, were children of God. But now that the so-called
Negros had to be cultivated into upstanding citizens, the missionaries
were given free rein to carry out their work.

Koos grew up on a plantation on the Commewijne River, right next
to a Catholic mission where a priest had set up a school for plantation
children. He was bright and eager to learn, but as a young black man,
the only future he had was in the infamous, malaria- and blackwater
fever–infested green hell. For as lucrative as gold mining could be, it
was extremely laborious and detrimental to one's health. Between the
dreaded jungle diseases, the use of mercury, and the hundreds of yards
of haphazardly built mineshafts, hardly any gowtumans lived to see
their fiftieth birthday.

The mix of African and indigenous blood pumping through Koos's
veins had produced a man of extremely tough constitution, and he
shared the character of the explorers who had once tamed the Wild
Coast. Koos was an energetic go-getter with big dreams. He meticu-
lously invested his earnings in new expeditions and Paramaribo real

estate, and at the dawn of the twentieth century, the twenty-eight-year-old "J. Th. G. Nods" prominently appeared on the list of eligible voters published in the annual *Gouvernements Advertentieblad*, thereby confirming he was among the wealthiest citizens. As is the case with most successful people, wealth alone wasn't enough for Koos. He wanted prestige. He wanted what was at that time and place the ultimate status symbol for a man of mixed race: a legal marriage with the whitest woman he could find.

On October 5, 1904, Koos triumphantly walked Eugenie under the king palm trees into the Lutheran church where he had just been accepted as a member that morning. Despite his skin color, he had made the most of the freedom he had been born into and the opportunities his homeland had to offer. He even adapted his occupation to his new life in Paramaribo's upper class. When they officially married in a civil ceremony at the Gouvernements Logeergebouw on December 14 of that year, he stated his profession as "writer," in other words, a civil servant—a highly respectable profession in Creole circles.

***

In September 1905, barely one year after her sensational wedding, Eugenie gave birth to a daughter, who was named Hilda Esline. The infant had her mother's relatively light skin, but the Creole features and round build of her African forefathers. Désiré Eugène, born in 1906, was a lighter version of his father: the same chiseled face, the same zest for life. With Waldemar Hugh, who entered the world on September 1, 1908, the Surinamese melting pot produced features that were nearly East Indian in appearance. The quartet was completed in 1910 with the birth of daughter Lily Mathilde, who won the genepool jackpot. The gods must have had a competition to unite the most stunning blend of features from the different races: thick black hair, light-brown skin, a heart-shaped face, and giant light-blue eyes, courtesy of her long-lost Scottish great-grandfather.

Waldemar and his brother and sisters were not destined to grow up as their father had—scrounging around barefoot on a languishing plantation for whatever he could get his hands on. The four of them had only the best in life. They were baptized in the silver font that a Dutch plantation family had once donated to the Lutheran church and were cared for by a real English nanny imported by their father from British Guiana. They lived on the elegant Heerenstraat in a mansion furnished with expensive carpets, furniture, porcelain, and crystal, and they were dressed in the most beautiful clothes and shoes that money could buy. They spent the hottest months of the year at their holiday house in Barbados, which they sailed to in a slender schooner their father had had custom built.

Although the Nods children were known to be friendly and well mannered, they had—as the members of the Paramaribo gossip mill would say with a puckered brow—their noses so high in the air they couldn't see the ground. Apparently, this didn't have so much to do with the way they talked or behaved, but more with the way they carried themselves and a look in their eyes. Because even though slavery was a thing of the past, the colony still held all things white in high esteem, and it wasn't so unusual for a lighter-skinned child to simply refuse to be seen on the street with a darker sibling. Everyone knew their place, or rather their color, and acted accordingly. But Waldemar and his brother and sisters held their heads high and looked the world straight in the eye as if they were members of Paramaribo royalty. But, of course—as people muttered under their breath—what else would you expect from such a father, who eschewed the kind of modesty expected from people born with his dark skin tone? Koos Nods was not about to take off his hat and bow his head and mumble "Yes, m'ster" and "No, m'ster" every time he crossed paths with a Dutch person.

Koos Nods carried himself like a gentleman, and, although entirely unsuitable for the tropical climate, dressed his wife in heavy brocades and velvet gowns. Together, they traveled around the Caribbean like rich European and American couples were in the habit of doing, and he raised his children to be princes and princesses. If he and Eugenie were still to be classified into the categories of the past, then their children were symbols of the country's entire remarkable history and its people. Their ancestors had come from every corner of the world, and they were just as much the descendants of slaves as they were of masters. The Nodses were children of the world, like everyone from Suriname.

***

In 1914, the Great War broke out in Europe, just as Suriname's golden economy was starting to lose its sparkle. One year before, with great pomp and circumstance, the final section of the 107-mile-long railroad from the center of Paramaribo to the goldfields in the south of the country was completed. But as fate would have it, the festive opening celebration was not the prelude to prosperity that everyone had expected. On the contrary, gold findings were becoming alarmingly fewer and further between, and in the meantime, the war was proving to be a painful reminder of how dependent Suriname still was on the Netherlands. As fewer European vessels made their way up the Suriname River, the shortage of basic commodities like flour and cloth became more acute. When, on top of that, the farms were hit by a wave of crop diseases, hunger became all too familiar in poor areas of the city.

Koos tried to turn the tides by investing in balata cultivation. Around the turn of the century, German researchers had discovered a process for extracting this natural rubber from the colony's wealth of balata trees. Granted, cultivating raw materials for transmission belts and insulation material was hardly as lucrative as striking gold, but it involved significantly less risk, and foreign companies were sending "balata bleeders" into the jungle by the thousands. As one of the few Surinamese among them, Koos Nods had both the money and the guts to outfit the rubber expeditions himself, and after a few successful expeditions to the east of the Suriname River, he organized a large-scale expedition into the Amazon basin in 1914. But this time, the luck that he had grown so used to having on his side failed him miserably. A large portion of his contract workers fell victim to jungle diseases, and the rest, having been left unattended for just a short while, ran off with the profits.

The adventure cost Koos a large portion of his fortune and forced him to move his family to the Waterfront in the commercial heart of Paramaribo, where they had a wide view over the Suriname River. The new address had perhaps less of the tranquil stateliness of the old one, but it was still quite prestigious. The Waterfront had been the beating heart of the colony since its early days. Every person who had made Suriname what it was had walked down the wooden docks that connected the colony to the rest of the world. Those jetties had borne the loud stomping boots of the European buccaneers who had disputed the territory, the patter of the finely embroidered slippers of the Jewish planters' wives, the thumping of the tattered soles of immigrants, and of course, the dull shuffle of tens of thousands of barefoot slaves.

The new Nods family residence was a white two-story wood house at number 76, raised in the middle with lower wings on either side. Located between the weighing house—officially known as De Waag—and the Creole market and directly on the rail line to the south, the house was ideally positioned for the expedition equipment shop that Koos opened on the ground floor. But Waldemar's father turned out to be far too restless to waste away behind a counter, and it wasn't long before he headed out again on his schooner, this time to Brazil in search of gold and precious stones. But what the children didn't know—and it is even unclear whether Eugenie knew—was that on his trip to Rio de Janeiro, he was accompanied by a woman seventeen years younger than he was, whom he had already married back in Paramaribo. However, he never divorced Eugenie. In a world where having multiple concubines was fully acceptable, he evidently assumed that the same norms applied to a legal spouse.

In the years that followed, Koos remained fully devoted to his first family. Every year he went with Eugenie and the children on holiday to Barbados and regularly sailed with his sons to the British colony of Trinidad to buy horses for their carriage in Paramaribo. But the Great War raged on, and the balata industry withered as a result of falling prices and overexploitation. Suriname's economic horizon grew dim. And the more he found his footing in rich Brazil, the less time he spent on the Waterfront. Because beneath the shiny exterior of upstanding citizen, Koos Nods was an adventurer at heart, a rolling stone who left behind anything he didn't need.

***

Waldemar, who was six when the family moved to the Waterfront, seemed to hardly notice his father's more frequent absences. He lived in a world of women: he had his mother; his caring sister, Hilda; his spoiled-rotten little sister, Lily; and their former nanny, May, who now reigned over the preschool he went to in the mornings. The floorboards of his new world on the river were painted red, the red of the brazilwood tree, and he could look out from the front balcony all day long without getting bored for a second. There was always something to see on the street below: carts rattling down the cobblestones, shouting street vendors peddling their wares, colorfully clad tribesmen and people of all races who came to the daily Creole market on the big, canoe-flanked dock known as the *agu tobo*, or the "pig trough."

Once a day, the steam train thundered by, sending thick clouds of soot out over the river. For the older boys, like Waldemar's rascal brother, Decy, jumping on the back of the cars and hanging on until the Waterfront branched off from the river was a favorite pastime. But especially during the dry season, the flying sparks would regularly cause fires—that was how an *omi sneisi*, a Chinese spice shop, burned to the ground. Waldemar's mother always had a few buckets of water ready in the front gallery.

To the left of their house, Waldemar could just make out the contour of Fort Zeelandia and the cannons that had been defending the coastline from invaders for as long as anyone could remember. In front of the fort were the sundial-crested marine stairs, where the governor welcomed the sloops from visiting marine vessels and tent boats carrying distinguished guests from Holland. The largest and most important docks were actually those behind De Waag, kitty-corner to the Nodses' house, where the river boats moored, and in more prosperous times, passengers from the European steamships disembarked.

In the evening, when the darkness suddenly set in, Waldemar would watch the lantern lighter use a long pole with a hook on the end to raise the gas mantle up to the street lanterns and set it aflame. In the warm glow, he could see the bats and moths circling around the blooming honeysuckle next to the house. In bed, he could hear bits of jazz carried by the wind from the cafés on the Saramacastraat and Dutch sailors singing their way back to their barracks in Fort Zeelandia. And on Sunday morning, when all the shops were closed, he could watch the entire city parade down the Waterfront. Even the whites, who were usually shut up in their dark houses or at their clubs, wouldn't miss the opportunity to catch up on the latest news and gossip and to see and be seen. And in the afternoon, everyone would head down to the main square, the Oranjeplein, to enjoy the weekly musical performance in front of the governor's palace next to the Palmtree Garden.

But what Waldemar found more beautiful than all of this, even more beautiful than the annual Queen's Day regatta, was the river itself. He could smell the briny sea, and the sky overhead was constantly changing—sometimes blue, with towering clouds that glided like sailboats over the water below, sometimes nearly white from the blistering heat, and sometimes so dark that suddenly he could no longer see the grayish-green strip of jungle on the other side. He could smell the rain coming before it came pelting down like a curtain—a *sibibusi* like that would wash the city squeaky clean. And once the storm had passed, the world would be bathed in the aroma of the pineapple plants and the lemon and tamarind trees that lined the wide sandy streets; and from the tops of the palm trees in the Palmtree Garden—which had looked so tired and dusty before the rain—fresh green blades would suddenly sprout.

The sight of Koos Nods's schooner bobbing in front of the house was becoming increasingly less frequent, but his absence wasn't so unusual. Fathers were hardly ever home; that's just the way it was. Most of Waldemar's black friends were raised exclusively by their mothers, and it was already considered tremendously chic to have someone in your life you could even call father, and even better if he was officially married to your mother. The fact that Waldemar and his siblings had all kinds of older half brothers around the city was never much of a secret. There was even one who had the same last name as they did, but he was a poor fieldworker outside the city, certainly not someone the fashionable children could be associated with.

In Waldemar's eyes, his father was an almost mythical character, a person who popped up in his life every now and then and told the most extraordinary tales of Brazil, where he owned a hotel and gemstone quarry, among other things, and lived as a grand seigneur. The only thing that Waldemar did notice about his father's gradual disappearance from their lives was the change in his mother. Eugenie became even more quiet than she already was, and she devoted more of her attention to him, the most dreamy eyed and affectionate of all her children.

***

On December 10, 1918, all of Paramaribo gathered on the Waterfront. The Great War was over, and for the first time in years, a Dutch ship was making its way up the Suriname River. The cannons at Fort Zeelandia welcomed the vessel with a thundering salute, and free loaves of bread were distributed on the Oranjeplein that afternoon to celebrate the

return of flour, and with it hope—hope for better times now that the
connection with the motherland had been restored.

But times did not get better. On the contrary, a few weeks later
an influenza epidemic spread across the city like wildfire and claimed
thousands of lives from the impoverished population. In the months
that followed, it became clear that the end of the war had come too late
to breathe new life into the colony's moribund economy. The goldfields
had gone dry, the price of natural rubber on the international market
had hit an all-time low, and Suriname's golden years were over. Almost
every year, the colonial government, the Koloniale Staten, was forced
to make the humiliating journey to Holland to balance the books.
Unemployment grew to unprecedented proportions, especially among
the Creoles, who faced formidable competition from the tens of thousands of Hindustani and Javanese migrants who had been lured to the
colony to work on the plantations after the abolishment of slavery.

Anyone who had the opportunity to leave did. Black men took
refuge in the Antilles or Venezuela, where there was good money to
be earned in the up-and-coming oil industry. People of mixed race
went to the Dutch East Indies, where the Netherlands Trading Society
was developing relatively well and was happy to hire the "Dutchified"
Surinamese. And the well-to-do went back to Holland, where industrialization was in full swing. Among them were many Jewish families
who had long been the backbone of the colony. After laws limiting
Jews were abolished in 1825, they gained even more influence in the
colony. Salomon Soesman, owner of Waldemar's grandmother Mietje,
had come to the colony as a young man from Amsterdam in 1826 and
managed to become one of the richest men in Suriname and the vice-
chairman of the Koloniale Staten. But after slavery was abolished, the
plantation world that had made Soesman so successful ended up being
his downfall. In his day, going back to Europe, like the other Dutch
were doing, was still deemed too dangerous for his people. But now,
in the enlightened twentieth century, the Jewish people didn't have as

much fear in the Old World. They headed back to Europe unperturbed about the future.

During this economically unstable time, Koos had completely disappeared from his homeland and left Eugenie alone in the big house on the Waterfront. She scraped by on the ever-dwindling rental income from the ground-floor tenants and her husband's last bits of real estate. When that was no longer enough, she sold her most tangible memories of her former luxury: her jewelry. After that, she tried to start a hotel. The house was certainly large enough, and in the old days, the location would have been ideal. But the quays that were once teeming with European visitors looking for a comfortable bed in a proper environment were now miserably empty. Investors were no longer willing to risk sinking their money into the bottomless pit on the other side of the ocean, and the officials that came to the door on the night of July 31, 1921, as part of the Great Census counted only one person at house number 76 who wasn't in the family—a boarder employed as a clerk.

But even though Eugenie was struggling to make ends meet, she and her children still did their best to live as members of the upper class. Sixteen-year-old Hilda had been courted by an engine driver in the merchant navy for years, but as the granddaughter of Grandma Elder, she had grown up all too aware of subtle differences in social status and refused him time and again. Even though they were now forced to rent out rooms in their home, they were still the Nods children, and a black shoemaker's son with frizzy hair was simply beneath her dignity. She preferred to help her mother by working as a grocery store bookkeeper. Every Saturday, even in the sweltering heat, the Nodses still ate calf's liver and potatoes. For even though the Dutch government was impatient to be rid of the poverty-stricken colony, and the people in Paramaribo were endlessly complaining about the arrogant, meddlesome penny-pinchers in The Hague, the motherland was still a symbol of the big world, the source of all knowledge and prosperity.

The Creole population was particularly devoted to the Kingdom of the Netherlands and its royal family. Even during the economic depression, when Queen Wilhelmina celebrated the silver jubilee of her reign in 1923, no other territory collected as much money for her gift as the one on the Suriname River. And it was still the dream of every Surinamese parent of standing to give his or her child a European education. Even Eugenie did everything in her power to make this dream from better times a reality; however, in the disillusioned Suriname of the 1920s, the costs of such an endeavor had become unfathomable. While an annual salary of 1,000 guldens was considered a decent living in the colony, a second-class ticket for the Atlantic crossing was at least 200 guldens, and in pricey Holland, living costs and school fees quickly added up to 175 guldens a month.

Decy turned out to be too much like his adventurous father to sit in school, and as soon as he turned sixteen, he left for Curaçao in search of the fortune that was so terribly hard to come by in his homeland. And so, it was up to his little brother, Waldemar, to make his mother's dream come true. Starting July 1, 1923, Waldemar attended the Hendrik School, the only school in the colony to offer an advanced elementary education certificate that would be recognized in Holland. The Hendrik School on the Gravenstraat had once been attended exclusively by rich children of plantation owners, wealthy Jews, and members of the Dutch elite. The only black people on the school premises were the servant girls who waited for their young masters by the gate, bearing trays with glasses of chocolate milk or lemonade—neatly covered with paper against the flies. But following the exodus in the second half of the nineteenth century, the institution became open to students of color, and in 1891 it admitted the first full-blooded African student. By then, more than half of the students and teachers at the Hendrik School were Creole.

This was by no means the end of racial discrimination in Suriname. Even though the Surinamese students were generally more well liked than their Dutch peers—who apparently made little effort to hide their disdain for this so-called monkey land they had found themselves in—they still enjoyed less prestige. Students were forbidden to speak "Negro English," a dialect spoken by many Creole Surinamese, and the lessons were an exact copy of those in the motherland. The rhythm of the Dutch school day was strictly adhered to—even though it was totally unsuitable in a tropical climate. If the teachers wished to teach their pupils anything about their own country, they were left entirely to their own devices. For example, when rain fell on the Petrea-vine-covered school grounds, a first-grade teacher might explain how little streams from the highlands made their way down to the sea and eventually came together to form big, wide rivers like the Suriname River and the Commewijne.

***

Waldemar was cheerful and took to school easily, but he didn't love studying. He preferred to roam the city with his friends. Even though the Pearl of the West had lost much of her golden sparkle, for young boys from the tropics like Waldemar, it was still a virtual Eldorado, an inexhaustible source of adventure and distraction. As soon as the clock on the famous wooden cathedral next to the school struck three, the rest of the day was theirs. They would head down to Bourne's on the Waterfront to look at cars, go fishing in the Sommelsdijk stream, or watch the big ships come in at Fort Zeelandia. They explored the green districts around the edge of the city, where the Javanese and *burus*, poor Dutch farmers who had been shipped to Suriname, worked in the fields, and where they could pick sweet mangos right off the trees. The only place they didn't dare go was into the impenetrable jungle beyond the fields, because, like most city-dwelling Creoles, they were in the habit of telling each other horror stories about all the wild animals and shady types roaming around in the trees. They were happier taking their boats upriver to fish, swim, and sail.

Waldemar's carefree life came to a screeching halt in 1924 when his mother was urgently rushed to the Catholic hospital on the Koninginnestraat. A few days later, Eugenie died of appendicitis. She was just fifty years old. After her children had laid her to rest at the Lutheran cemetery on the Wanicastraat, the house on the Waterfront was vacated. Waldemar and his sisters moved in with their aunt Marie in her stately home on the Wagenwegstraat. Eugenie's sister was married to a civil servant and therefore among those who had suffered the least during the crisis. She was known for being a rather cold woman, but in her own undemonstrative way, she took excellent care of her nieces and nephews. To his four little cousins, Waldemar was like a wonderful big brother; he even let them borrow his long trousers so they could sneak past the age limit at the cinema. In July 1926, Waldemar took his final exams. Two months later, he and his fellow graduates rode through Paramaribo in a honking convertible, and he began preparing to fulfill his mother's dying wish.

His entire childhood, Waldemar had seen them go, the ocean swimmers envied by all. And now he himself was one of the young men headed off to Holland, off to a promising future. Hilda had made arrangements for his arrival on the other side. It turned out that their father had conceived a son with a married mistress who had moved back to the motherland ten years before. The son, David Millar, had written that he was prepared to take care of his half brother on the condition that, if anyone asked, he would say he was a nephew.

On Saturday morning, October 22, 1927, Waldemar was taken by family and friends in a small boat to the Belwaarde docks, where the boilers of the *Oranje Nassau* were already generating steam for the great crossing. Waldemar knew the ship well. He and his friends had often hung around the stern in their little boat. The ship, which was approximately 328 feet long and could accommodate about sixty passengers, was the property of the Royal Dutch Steamboat Company, which had recently taken over the four-week Holland–Suriname line.

It had been at sea for two months already and now, having left the New York and West Indian ports, it was on its way back to its home port in Amsterdam. Around noon came the shrill sound of the steam whistle and the rattle of anchors being pulled up.

Slowly the ship came to life, and Waldemar glided away from the only world he had ever known. The farewell cries of the people on the quay were gradually overpowered by the soft monotone drone of the engines churning in the belly of the ship, and soon enough the sight of their waving arms had disappeared as well. Paramaribo sparkled white in the bright sun, the trees on the Waterfront looked dusty, and the riverbank seemed as endless and impenetrable as ever. Every now and then, the passengers might have caught a glimpse of an old white plantation house peeking through the green or a whiff of blooming mahogany trees and burning wood carried to the deck by the wind. After a few miles, Fort New Amsterdam was in sight, and as always, the boat let off a final farewell signal, rousing the screaming monkeys in the surrounding jungle. But this time there were other boys untying their boat and waving goodbye to the passengers, and Waldemar could no longer dive into the water and let the rising tide carry him home. He watched them follow the ship until the river's sandy waters swirled into the ocean's blue. The ship was headed north-northeast—away from the sun and into the falling darkness.

***

The journey began splendidly. Although it was still very warm, the sea breeze was cool and pleasant; the smooth, blue Atlantic Ocean stretched out as far as the eye could see. Flying fish skimmed across the surface of the water like silver stars, and every now and then, glistening dolphins would swim alongside the boat. For a while, the passengers could still make out the low coastline of the Guianas. Somewhere in that far-off strip of monotone green was the crumbling, forgotten plantation where Waldemar's family came from, and where his half-Indian great-grandmother, Prinzes, and her mother, Aurora, were still buried in the slave graveyard that had long been overgrown by the jungle.

Every morning, the sun rose a little bit earlier, and the ship's clocks were set forward; and every evening it would go down a bit earlier in the ship's wake. After a few days, the *Oranje Nassau* left the Caribbean and ventured forth into the Middle Passage, as seafarers called the infamous intercontinental crossing. The ship more or less followed the same route the European slave traders had taken centuries earlier, their wooden vessels full of human misery—the misery of the suffocating slaves crammed into the belly of the ship, and the misery of the poor devils working as sailors, who were even less likely to make it home alive. Unlike their human cargo below deck, their lives weren't worth a penny.

But death was aboard the *Oranje Nassau* as well. At about latitude 25° north, when storm clouds formed in the clear blue sky and white-crested waves—or "white horses" as the sailors called them—appeared on the sea, a forty-year-old Danish passenger died of malaria. Just a few months earlier, she and her family had come to Suriname full of hope. Like so many immigrants who'd gone before them, they were naive and totally unprepared for the extreme tropical climate and terrible economic situation that awaited them. At the peak of Suriname's biannual dry period, she had become so sick and feverish in the scorching heat that her husband and two children scraped together all the money they had and booked their tickets on the first ship away from the godforsaken land and home to the mild, green hills of Denmark—hills that Mrs. Ericson would never see again.

Death on board was bad luck, everyone knew that, and preparations were quickly made for a burial at sea. But when Mrs. Ericson's husband and children got wind of the plans to relinquish her body to the waves, they protested: if she was to be thrown overboard, they would go down with her. There were no cold stores on the ship, and in the end, the captain had no choice but to assign the ship's doctor the unpleasant task of preserving the body in alcohol and salt and stowing it away on the highest deck.

In the Bay of Biscay, a furious storm broke out. The ship was thrashed about for days on end. Anything that wasn't battened down rolled back and forth, and when Waldemar walked from his cabin to the passengers' mess hall, he had to hold on for dear life. By then the coffin was emitting an intolerable odor that could be smelled all over the ship. Once they entered the English Channel, the wind died down a bit. Still carrying the macabre cargo, the *Oranje Nassau* plowed through the leaden waves at top speed. The superstitious sailors wanted nothing more than to step off the ill-fated ship as soon as possible, and they did everything they could to limit the stopovers in Plymouth and Le Havre to an absolute minimum. Counting down the days until they reached the Suriname quay in the Port of Amsterdam, passengers tried to ignore the smell of death in their nostrils.

The ship arrived in the IJmuiden locks four days ahead of schedule. The first thing Waldemar saw in his new country was the dunes rising up on the gray horizon, and the flat, soggy pastures on either side of the North Sea Canal. Shivering, he stood at the railing in his elegant tropical jacket, which was far too thin for this new climate. His brown skin looked sallow in the northern light. It was November by the time he arrived in rainy, windy Holland. The last leaves clung to their branches, and the people hurried down the wet streets seeking shelter and a place to call home.

3

The Boarder

From the moment Waldemar set foot on shore, the promised land he and his friends had imagined while swinging in the lithe branches of the guava trees was different than he had expected. In fact, his first steps on Dutch ground ended up being delayed for days, for as soon as the *Oranje Nassau* moored on the Surinamekade in Amsterdam, the Danish passengers began shouting for the police. When the authorities finally arrived, the family reported a murder, claiming that the ship's doctor had failed to provide their wife and mother with proper treatment. Her corpse, which was in an advanced state of decomposition by then, was proof. No one could leave the ship while the investigation was underway, and it was nearly a week before Waldemar was picked up by his "uncle" David Millar and taken to The Hague.

The boy from Paramaribo had landed in a strange new world. The trees were so bare they seemed dead. The streets and stoops looked as though they'd been drawn with a ruler, and—perhaps most remarkable of all—white people did jobs that even black people would turn their noses up at in Suriname, like collecting trash and sweeping the street.

Everything was different in Holland. Even the moon stood up straight in the sky rather than sprawling out over the sea like it did at home.

The climate was cold, and the people were even colder. David's wife, for example, was oddly cool toward Waldemar. No matter how polite and quiet he was, Christien managed to find something wrong with everything he said and did. Even her two children acted peculiarly— they seemed a bit afraid of him and crawled under the table whenever he tried to play with them. As for David Millar, he had very little time for his half brother, and whenever he was home, he was short-tempered because of stress at work.

Most Surinamese who came to the Netherlands settled in Amsterdam, a loose, cosmopolitan city where they could find plenty of compatriots in the sailor bars around the Zeedijk and in the neighborhoods around the harbor. A thriving Surinamese community was emerging in Amsterdam around that time, which included a workers' union, the Bond van Surinaamse Arbeiders in Nederland, and cultural associations such as the Vereniging Ons Suriname. But The Hague had neither the ambience nor the nightlife to make people from the West Indies feel at home. What's more, differences in class traveled with the ship. Although Surinamese men were all equally black in Dutch eyes, among themselves the social differences in the colony were still perfectly apparent, and a black university student wouldn't dream of fraternizing with a black engine driver.

Though the Nods family had lost much of its wealth over the years, Waldemar had always been counted among Paramaribo's social elite. But in Holland, he was suddenly nothing more than a poor black immigrant surrounded by European wealth. All the guldens his family had worked so hard to scrape together for him would have constituted a fortune back home, but here they were barely enough to put warm clothes on his back.

In his host family, Waldemar was clearly unwelcome; in his university preparatory course, he was an outsider; and on the street, he was an object of curiosity. Sometimes people secretly tried to touch him to see if his dark pigment would rub off, and in the tram, children stared at him as if he were the bogeyman himself. Dumbfounded, Waldemar spent his first year in Holland wandering the endless streets and housing blocks of The Hague. No one knew him, and no one seemed to want to know him. He became shy and unsure of himself and, above all, extremely lonely.

Even the summer couldn't cure Waldemar's homesickness for Paramaribo, the breeziness of tropical life, and the river. The colors of the Dutch flowers looked pale in his eyes, and just as it finally seemed to be warming up outside, autumn announced its return. When Christien told him that he would be moving in with her cousin, who had just started a boarding house, he had already given up all hope that things would ever get better for him. By then, it was November again, and he had neither the clothes nor the spirit to face the winter.

***

On Tuesday morning, November 20, 1928, Rika and her children moved into the upstairs apartment of the house on Azaleastraat. Waldemar moved in with them that same day. About three weeks after the move, Rika had a photographer take their family portraits for the annual Sinterklaas celebration. The children all looked sadly into the camera. Having been torn away from the island and their friends, they still weren't used to their new life. Their mother looked serious, albeit a bit slimmer and calmer than in the photos taken earlier that year. Having her own house brought a sense of stability, and now she had not only her children to shower with warmth and care but the boarder as well. Although Waldemar looked exotic with his dark skin, he soon became a familiar face in the house, if only because she cooked his meals, washed his clothes, and changed his bedsheets. Rika found their house guest much too skinny for his height, so she learned how to cook rice just for him and drenched it in the same gravy the rest of the family poured over their potatoes.

Waldemar flourished in Rika's slightly chaotic but cheerful household. He enjoyed the buzz of a large family and had endless patience for the children, who listened with jaws dropped to his stories about the wonderfully warm country he came from, where the leaves stayed on the trees, you never needed heavy clothes, and you could go swimming every single day. If his landlady turned on the radio, he'd get a twinkle in his eye, and sometimes they dared to dance. And in the evenings, after the children were in bed, Rika enjoyed having another adult in the house to talk to. True, he was quite a bit younger than she was, but he was a good listener and showed an uncommon understanding for her plight. And there was no denying that he was an attractive man, especially now that he was slightly heftier and opening up a bit.

"White women are softer," Waldemar and his friends back home had concluded in one of their worldly-wise conversations about the opposite sex. During his first year in Holland, Waldemar had serious doubts about whether this was actually true; however, during those late-night conversations on the Azaleastraat, he may have started to believe it. His landlady was unarguably loving and warm. She even reminded him of his own mother, who, despite having been poorly treated by her husband and ending up alone, had always been kind and helpful to everyone. Rika's zest for life and independent nature made her not unlike Surinamese women, and even though she was quite a bit older than he was, she had always been a robust, attractive woman—even more so now that she was taking better care of herself and able to look at him with a smile in her eyes.

One wintery day in January 1929, the landlady and her boarder photographed each other on the Azaleastraat in the freshly fallen snow. Both had clearly dressed up for the occasion. With his suit, elegant hat, light raincoat, and a cigarette in hand, Waldemar looks straight out of one of the portraits of elegant Surinamese men that Dutch artist Nola

Hatterman was painting at the time. Rika poses coquettishly for the camera in her fur-trimmed overcoat, and something in her gaze suggests that her relationship with Waldemar is no longer strictly platonic. One month after the photos were taken, that was most certainly the case, for it must have been early spring when she realized that she was pregnant again—and the only man who could have possibly been the father was her young black boarder.

Abortion was illegal in those days, but still widely practiced. The fact that Rika chose to keep the baby, despite the strong social stigma against mixed-race relationships, says something about her feelings for the father. In quiet, caring Waldemar, she found what she'd been missing in her marriage: a man who supported her and who would never try to force his will upon her. She was in love and determined to share her life with him. Meanwhile, Willem Hagenaar still hadn't agreed to a divorce. He had applied for a job in the Dutch East Indies, perhaps in the hope that he and his family could start over in the colonies, where Rika could enjoy the kind of easygoing atmosphere and thriving social life he assumed she wanted. But to her, the news that her legal husband had a mind to leave the country came as a relief—it would certainly make her future with her still-secret lover a little bit easier.

For once, Rika's fluctuating weight turned out to be a godsend. She simply wore the dresses from her heavier days and trusted that by the time the pregnancy became visible, her children would be as attached to Waldemar as she was. Her oldest son, in particular, was really getting along with his new housemate. Wim regarded Waldemar as a kind of special friend, someone who had seen the world and with whom he could go on manly adventures. In the summer of 1929, the two of them went on a long camping trip together by tandem bicycle. Much to his delight, Wim got to ride in the front. At Jan's first communion, the rest of the Van der Lans family met Rika's boarder as well. They had nothing but positive things to say about him—what a nice young man, and so refined!

As for Waldemar, he didn't see anything standing in the way of a relationship with his landlady. In the Surinamese culture, sexual relations were simply not as big of a deal as they were in Holland, and a woman having children from more than one man was considered the most normal thing in the world. Even a considerable difference in age would not have been a major issue back home. And so, that summer he spent day after day with Rika and her children at the beach in Scheveningen, where he perfected the art of open-water swimming and became even darker than he already was. In early September, he celebrated his twenty-first birthday. For the first time since he had arrived in Holland, he felt happy. He came of age just in time for the birth of his child.

***

The beautiful summer gave way to a bleak fall, full of rain and wind. Wim, who had recently turned fourteen, started feeling less and less at ease. He was a sensitive boy, and as the oldest in the family, he had borne the brunt of his parents' quarreling and all the problems his mother had created for herself since she left his father. He had always been the apple of his mother's eye, and in The Hague, he became her anchor. He did his best to be the man of the family, but now he was getting caught up in something he couldn't quite understand. Hushed voices behind closed doors, music playing deep into the night, quiet giggles in the hall, waking up in the morning to the smell of smoke and empty glasses downstairs. And a mother who was so visibly and imperturbably happy, even though she seemed to be getting heavier by the day. At the beginning of October, Rika finally confided in her oldest son: pretty soon he would have a new baby brother or sister. And the best part—the baby would have brown skin, like his friend Waldemar.

In all her romantic optimism, perhaps Rika thought that the friendship between her son and lover would make things easier. Sadly, this was not the case. The adolescent Wim was deeply hurt. He was at an age when he was just starting to understand the physical powers of attraction between a man and a woman, and he found the thought of his mother and the boarder revolting. He felt intensely betrayed, not only by Rika, but by Waldemar—he had been so friendly toward him, but all the while he'd secretly been after his mother. "The brown kids are coming, and there'll be no more room for us!" he cried, and refused to exchange another word with the two of them.[9]

That Sunday, Wim was on acolyte duty at the church. He emptied the contents of his piggy bank and tucked a copy of the Dutch Civil Code into his white surplice. Halfway through the procession, he disappeared into the crowd and met up with his eight-year-old brother, Jan, at a previously agreed location. Together, they took the train to Rotterdam and then the tram to Hellevoetsluis, where they boarded the boat to Goeree. By the time they reached the island, Wim had run out of money, but he managed to borrow some from one of his father's employees. They took the last tram to Goedereede. That evening, the two boys found themselves standing before the dumbfounded dike warden, who was even more shocked when his oldest son opened the Civil Code and gravely pointed to a passage stating that a father was required to care for his children.

When Willem finally connected the dots in his son's jumbled story and understood why the two boys no longer wanted to live with their mother, he snapped. Not only were his hopes for reconciliation with Rika shattered, the news stirred up his white man's fear of the black man's virility—the same fear that centuries earlier had compelled the colonists to declare relations between white women and slaves punishable by death. In the days that followed, Willem arranged for his oldest son to return to school as soon as possible, withdrew his application for the position in the Indies, and informed his wife via a hastily contracted lawyer that he was going to do everything in his power to remove his other two children from her damaging influence.

The news spread through The Hague society like wildfire. Rika, a married woman, had taken up with a black man young enough to be her son and was about to give birth to a brown bastard baby. It was a scandal of incalculable proportions. For Mr. and Mrs. Van der Lans, who had already had their hands full with Rika, this was the final straw. They cut their daughter out of their lives and hearts completely. Other family members severed ties with her as well. Even her brothers and sisters, who had always enjoyed, and sometimes even admired, their independent sister's antics, wanted nothing more to do with her.

***

On November 17, 1929, almost two years to the day that Waldemar set foot in Amsterdam, his son was born. In Surinamese terms, the baby was a real *moksi-moksi*: brown with dark curls and bright blue eyes. Rika, whose last name was still officially Hagenaar, was not allowed to give her son his father's last name, but she did give him his first name. Little Waldemar soon became Waldy for short, but Rika liked to call him "Sonny Boy," after the sentimental song sung by Al Jolson in the popular film *The Singing Fool*, which everyone was whistling that summer.

> When there are grey skies
> I don't mind the grey skies
> You make them blue, Sonny Boy[10]

That winter, Willem made one last hopeless attempt to save his marriage. He told his wife he would take her back and would accept little Waldy as well. For someone as proud and bullheaded as he was, it was the ultimate sacrifice, but for Rika, his offer wasn't even worth considering. After nearly twenty years, the passionate love affair between Willem Hagenaar and Rika van der Lans had come to a bitter end, and an all-out war was inevitable. Willem spent a year's salary on lawyers

to gain custody of his two youngest children, while Rika did everything she could to regain contact with her two oldest sons. But all her
attempts were thwarted, not only by their father, but by her own family.
As her daughter, Bertha, later noted in her diary:

> I suddenly remember Mama coming to Grandpa's to
> visit. We weren't living with Papa yet. Only Wim and
> Jan. Grandpa said: Get out of here or I will! Wim and
> Jan never even came [to see us]. I stood in front of
> Grandpa and said: I'm leaving, you go back inside. I
> took my coat and Henk with me and went home with
> Mama, even though they were my own brothers. We
> were strangers to each other.[11]

For the first time in her life, Rika, who had always been a spoiled
daughter of the bourgeoisie, found herself in a bitter state of poverty.
It wasn't that money had never been in short supply growing up, but
her father had always managed to make some kind of lucrative transac-
tion that provided them with cash in abundance. She then spent her
marriage nestled under the wings of the Rijkswaterstaat, in a luxurious
home with an ample income and even a few servant girls of her own.
But without her family and husband, she had to watch every penny she
spent. She sold her jewelry and everything else of value she owned and
mended Waldemar's threadbare suits and shirts until they were literally
falling apart—so he could attend class looking as dignified as possible.
She even tried to earn money telling fortunes, which had always been
a favorite pastime of hers. And when things got really tight, and her
children were going to bed with growling, empty stomachs, she would
rent her rooms by the hour to couples.

On March 31, 1930, in The Hague's circuit court, Willem officially
denied that he was the father of Rika's mixed-race love child. Shortly
afterward, Rika, beaten down by lack of money and the dead-end

situation, gave up the fight. It had become clear to her that no judge was going to grant custody to an adulterous wife and her student lover who didn't even have the means to care for their own baby. Perhaps, she reasoned, it would even be better for her older children to grow up together with their father in that beautiful house on the island, where faithful Jans would surely see to it that all their material needs were cared for. Then they could spend their vacations with their mother and half brother.

Bertha was allowed to finish out the school year in The Hague, but on June 2, a chaplain from Rika's church brought Bertha and four-year-old Henk back to Goeree.

> I still remember that on the last night before I left I got
> out of bed and asked Mama: Is it really the last night?
> The suitcase was lying there next to my bed. Mama
> said: "Sis, try to get used to it and write me anything
> that's in your heart." I went back to bed. But then I
> started to cry, and I couldn't stop. I felt so empty.[12]

Years later, Rika would confess in a letter to Henk that letting him and her other children go was the biggest mistake of her life. "I never should have done it," she wrote.[13]

***

On October 29, 1929, a few weeks before little Waldy was born, the New York stock market crashed, bringing an abrupt end to the prosperous, carefree 1920s. By March the following year, more than eighteen million people were out of work. The Depression spread around the world like an oil slick. In Suriname, it was a final death blow to the already ill-fated economy and to any hopes the local people had of a brighter future; in the Netherlands, it struck like a thunderstorm at the end of a beautiful summer day, delivering one unexpected blow after another while everyone trembled and tried to find shelter.

Waldemar and Rika had no work, no money, and no friends. The fact that Rika had sent off her own flesh and blood to live with their father so she could be free to gallivant with her lover—or at least that was the version of the story circling around The Hague—had drained any remaining credit she might have had in the family circle. All Rika and Waldemar had was the baby and each other; there wasn't a soul who would give them a cent—and this wasn't just because of their difference in age and culture; it was also due to the belief that black men weren't ones to stick around. Sooner or later, the handsome young black man would be off in search of greener pastures, leaving Rika and her mixed-race baby to beg on the streets, or worse.

By the summer of 1930, Rika and Waldemar had fallen so far behind on their rent that they were evicted from the house on Azaleastraat. The only person who couldn't bear to see them out on the streets was Rika's sister, Jo. She agreed to take the young family in until Waldemar had earned enough degrees for a fighting chance on the job market. He had given up on his preuniversity program by then and was trying to earn a degree in business correspondence as quickly as possible as well as pass the practical exams in commercial science. But no matter how tight things were for Rika and Waldemar, there was one thing they would not sacrifice: the parcels for Rika's children in Goedereede. Week after week, the fat envelopes addressed in Rika's elegant handwriting arrived on the island, often packed with dried flowers, as Rika wrote: "I can't live without flowers and sweet children."[14] For Henk, who couldn't read yet, she sent postcards with pictures of Shirley Temple and Queen Astrid. She wrote about her daily life in a tone far more cheerful than her situation actually was and always asked for details about the children's lives, as if they had only been apart for a few days rather than almost an entire year.

Tell Henk he better be good because Mama is saving
up for a pretty box of stationery. And Sis, you're back
to school again now, aren't you? Did you like sleeping
late?? You did, didn't you? I've been looking forward
to a postcard from your field trip all week. Or didn't
it happen? Don't get too crazy on your bicycle. Now
you can really enjoy this beautiful weather on it. Let
me know soon if you moved up a class in school.
And what are you playing on the piano—any little
pieces yet? That's wonderful, Sis, I would be absolutely
delighted to hear you play sometime. My handwriting
isn't very good, is it? The little one is on the floor right
now playing at my feet.[15]

Once a month, Rika splurged on a roll of film for Waldemar's only
luxury: his Leica camera. The best prints were invariably sent to Goeree,
most of them with captions on the back: "Think of us often!" Or: "For
my sweet Sis—Little Waldy having a ball while his papa tries to snap
a nice picture of him." The dozens of photos Rika sent to Goeree are
a montage of the new life that Rika had so desperately wanted her
children to be a part of. But at the same time, they were also a protest against a divorce that was turning out to be much more definitive
than she ever could have imagined, for the deeply wounded Willem
Hagenaar was absolutely determined to erase the woman he had once
loved so passionately from his life and the lives of his children. Rika had
forfeited her maternal rights when she gave up the custody battle, and
Willem had done everything in his power to keep her visitation rights
to an absolute minimum: two hours once a year at a neutral location—
not her house. Once, when her longing for her children became too
much to bear, Rika traveled to Goeree, but the adventure turned out
to be such a drama that she thought it better for the children not to
do it again.

In early 1931, Waldemar passed both of his exams, and David Millar found work for him in the bookkeeping department of a Dutch mortgage lender, the Hollandsche Hypotheekbank. His starting salary was only 200 guldens a month, not nearly enough to feed a family, but in those dark times it was a small wonder that he had found any work at all. That year, he and Rika bounced from address to address, staying at each one until they fell so far behind on rent that they were forced to steal away like thieves in the night. And putting another roof over their heads was no easy feat—not only due to their limited budget, but also because no self-respecting landlord wanted the burden of housing an unmarried couple, let alone a poor, black apprentice bookkeeper, his significantly older mistress, and their baby, who was shameless living proof of his parents' socially unacceptable love affair.

In that sense, it was hardly by chance that Rika and Waldemar finally ended up in Scheveningen, the former fishing village that, ever since the arrival of bathing culture and the opening of the Kurhaus Hotel in 1885, had been transformed into a fashionable seaside resort with international allure. In 1901, the Queen Wilhelmina Promenade pier was opened by Prince Hendrik himself. The town's main boulevard was lined with renowned establishments like the Grand Hotel, the Savoy, and Hotel Rauch, and on a beautiful day, all of The Hague would head down to the seaside for a stroll. But underneath all the cosmopolitan chicness, Scheveningen still functioned as the underbelly of The Hague, the gutter that picked up everything that didn't belong in the dignified royal city. It was home to Jewish people who had been chased out of Eastern Europe and Antwerp during the Great War, and former emigrants to the Dutch Indies who, upon return, had struggled to find their bearings in the bourgeois lifestyle of The Hague.

Rika and Waldemar both recovered in the salty air and bright light of the liberal seaside town. Rika was calmed by the sound of the waves, the broad horizon, and the eternal rhythm of the surf, and Waldemar, the swimmer, had the sea in his veins. His grandmother Mietje had loved to tell stories about the cotton plantation on the shores of the great ocean where she grew up, where you could always hear the sound of the sea. In fact, the people who lived on the Dageraad and the Dankbaarheid plantations were so content there that even after the abolishment of slavery, they fought together with their former master for years to save the plantations from collapse. In Scheveningen, Waldemar's homeland didn't seem as far away as in the concrete jungle of The Hague, where he had always felt out of place. If he closed his eyes, he could almost imagine he was back in Paramaribo, especially on warm summer days, when the waves crashing lazily on the shore seemed to turn into the sloshing of his beloved river, and the fishermen's trawlers almost sounded like the steamboats churning upstream back home.

In October 1931, Waldemar's oldest sister came to Holland. Hilda had finally succumbed to the engine driver's advances, and the couple planned to marry in The Hague before heading to the Dutch East Indies. Like most people from Suriname, she had always imagined Holland as a land of milk and honey and was deeply shocked to find her youngest brother and his family living in such a state of poverty. On top of that, the promised land wasn't nearly as wonderful as she had expected. That autumn, the first massive protests against rising unemployment were taking place in Holland's major cities. Crown Princess Juliana had appointed herself head of a crisis committee, and rich citizens were raising money to help the poor. But crisis was inevitable: no one was making a profit anymore, bankruptcies were on the rise, and the sad lines in front of the unemployment benefit offices were getting longer by the day. The storm was raging, and no one was safe from its wrath.

And it was cold! In a portrait taken that November, Hilda looks nearly frozen in her winter coat and wool gloves, with tears in her eyes. A little while later, she married Jo Herdigein, and the next day they stepped onto the boat to Palembang and set sail in search of the sweet colonial life that had become unattainable both in Suriname and in Holland. That winter, Rika and Waldemar moved to a house in

the heart of Scheveningen that was large enough for them to realize
their dream of starting a guesthouse. Because if one thing was clear,
under the current economic circumstances, there would be no future
for Waldemar at the mortgage lender.

In May 1932, the first guests arrived at Pension Nods, Rika's elegant
name for what was in reality a rather spartan guestroom. Fortunately, the
three young Germans on a bicycle holiday were used to little in the way
of luxury, as their own country had been hit even harder by the crisis
than the rest of the world following its humiliating defeat in the First
World War. Their satisfaction was evident in the hostess's guest book.
In the long marbled notebook, they wrote: "We were very happy with
the room and food."[16] And they weren't the only ones. It turned out that
Rika had a talent for making guests feel welcome and at home. It was
as if she bestowed all the motherly love she couldn't give to her older
children on her guests, who stayed for both short and longer periods of
time. One grateful vacationer wrote: "After an exhausting day, I came
back to find not a guesthouse, but a warm, cozy home."[17]

As for Rika, she fervently hoped that she would soon be able to
welcome her four older children in her new home. In her letters to
them, she even attempted to make peace with Willem:

> Do your best in your studies, Bertha. Always be thank-
> ful that Papa is successful in his work. Take good care
> of Henkie. He certainly loves Jans, now that he knows
> how nice she is to him. I'm happy about that. Study
> hard, be a very good girl and make Papa proud. Give
> your brothers a big hug from me. Waldy sends lots of
> kisses to all of you and warm greetings to Papa. Write
> back soon and say hi to Jans for me.[18]

Signed: "Your loving mother," with a thick line under "loving." As
the months turned into years, and there was no attempt at reconciliation

from Goedereede, Rika's stubborn cheerfulness took on an increasingly desperate undertone. She yearned for quick replies, contact, and most of all, the chance to see her children: "Ask Papa if you can all come stay with me for a little while over the holidays. I miss you so much."[19]

But of all the guests who showed up at Pension Nods, Rika's children were never among them. Willem Hagenaar had been born and raised on irreconcilability—his parents successfully spent the final years of their marriage without exchanging a single word with one another—and he accepted his responsibility with that same sense of scrupulousness. He revealed himself to be a dutiful and loving father, but also incredibly strict. The fact that their servant Jans was by now functioning as the semiofficial woman of the house in more ways than one was carefully kept secret from the children and the other people in the village. And as for the real Mrs. Hagenaar—she simply no longer existed, and anyone foolish enough to so much as mention her name would be met with Willem's icy gaze or swept into one of his fits of rage.

The two older boys had little trouble adjusting to their father's strict household. Wim, by then eighteen, had changed a lot since that dramatic fall of 1929. Before then, he had been a mild-mannered boy who would rather sit outside staring at the clouds than focus on his schoolwork. But since he returned to Goeree, he had applied himself more in school and had taken up a rational, even cynical, manner. He didn't want anything to do with his traitorous mother, nor could he muster up much respect for his father, who had let it all happen. He studied like a demon possessed, with one goal in mind: to get as far away as he could from his vain, egotistical parents, who had made such a mess of their lives and marriage. For Jan, who turned twelve in 1933, life was simpler: he simply followed his big brother, just like he did on that Sunday in 1929 when the two boys made a run for it. The fact that he had been able to go back to wandering the island to his heart's content more than made up for his mother's absence in his life. Following

Wim's lead, he ignored all her attempts toward reconciliation. He didn't read Rika's letters and refused to visit her.

The only one who dared to defy their father and maintain contact with their mother was Bertha. She was twelve when she left her mother, old enough to remember her and old enough to have become attached to her new baby brother. She had even become a bit close with friendly Waldemar. Bertha was always oscillating between loyalty to her father and missing her mother, but what seemed to cause her the most suffering was the fact that the latter was so taboo at home. In her diary, she wrote:

> How are they doing in Scheveningen? I often find myself longing for them.
>
> Today is Mama's birthday. They are probably celebrating it right now. What a pity I can't be there. I hope that all this doesn't go on too much longer. I long for Mama. I know that no one is thinking about her in this house. I will try my best. I want to move on, and I want to try to earn some money, so if Mama is ever in trouble, I can help her. I want to be free, wherever I go.[20]

Bertha faithfully kept her mother abreast of the ups and downs of her and her brothers' lives. She also made sure that Henk—who was only five when he had been taken away from Rika and could barely remember her—scribbled her a letter from time to time. On December 5, on the eve of Sinterklaas, an uncomfortable silence fell over the house when there was one last big package from The Hague to be opened. It was Bertha who set the box on the table and unwrapped it, fingers trembling. Little Henk was unable to resist the temptation of another present, but Wim and Jan made a show of averting their gaze and left the presents their mother had worked so hard for lying on the table.

***

In the spring of 1933, Waldemar and Rika moved yet again, this time to the first floor of an elegant house with a white colonial-style veranda, not far from the boulevard in Scheveningen. In fact, the house was too expensive for them, but Rika figured the investment would pay for itself as it was undeniably a much more attractive address for beachgoing guests. The new place was "at the seaside!!" as she triumphantly wrote in her letters. And indeed, on a clear day, if you stood on the balcony above the **Rooms for Rent** sign that Waldemar had hammered on, you could just make out a tiny strip of blue at the end of the street. Rika advertised that room as having a "a sea view."

She decorated the house in a tropical theme, with white wicker furniture, wooden blinds, and lush green plants. She was so proud of the result that she couldn't resist showing it to her daughter and Henk when they came for their annual visit to The Hague.

> Mama had sent a car and the two Waldys were sitting inside. Now I had promised Papa that I wouldn't go to Scheveningen. I told them so too. I'm not getting in the car. I stood there in front of it. The driver said, "Come on, make your mother happy and just get in." In the end, I didn't have a choice. "We're just going for a little drive through Rotterdam," Mama said. But once they got me in the car, they went to Scheveningen anyway. I cried all afternoon. I felt so alone again. Anyway, I told Papa everything.[21]

Willem was furious when Bertha told him that she and Henk had gone to their mother's house even though he had strictly forbidden them to do so. He sent his wife a stern letter. She had demonstrated, once again, how untrustworthy she was and as a result, next year's visit would be cancelled. Only then did Rika realize, perhaps for the first time, that Willem would take his grudge against her to the grave and that she had truly lost her children.

The divorce dragged on for years, and the relentless negative propaganda eventually took its toll on Bertha, and her letters became shorter and less frequent. Although Bertha often endured periods of indefinable sadness, "the nostalgic feeling," as she called it, she began writing more about how she missed having *a* mother, rather than *her* mother.[22]

> It's strange, but I think about Mama much less than
> I did before. When I used to think about her, I imag-
> ined her with her hair in a bun, still so long, and wear-
> ing a dark dress or a white pinafore with long sleeves.
> But I don't see her that way in my mind anymore.
> Now when I think of Mama, I see her with short
> hair and fancy silk dresses, and I always smell eau de
> cologne.[23]

Nevertheless, Rika's long, loving letters arrived at the Rijkswaterstaat residence in Goedereede every week, and she continued to spend every cent she could spare on photos and presents for her four older children. However, she had given up all hope of a quick reunion. Having fully understood that it would take years before she would have the chance to rebuild a normal relationship with her children, she channeled her boundless energy into the one thing she did have control over, her one escape from the misery of losing them: her guesthouse.

"I'm like a dog on the prowl, always on the lookout for beach guests to welcome with open arms,"[24] she once wrote, explaining that the reason she didn't dare leave her post for fear of missing guests passing by was that she didn't have a telephone connection. Every guest that entered Pension Nods was showered with tremendous warmth, as a young Englishman wrote in the guest book in July 1933:

> My university friend and I have spent two weeks at
> the Academy of International Law and have had a very
> enjoyable time here. We had such a wonderful stay in
> Holland. Nothing was spared to make us both com-
> fortable and happy.[25]

Meanwhile, the number of unemployed people in the Netherlands had risen above three hundred thousand, Prime Minister Colijn's cabinet was imposing one draconian spending cut after another, and even the expensive hotels along the boulevard were struggling to keep their rooms occupied. But, time and again, Rika managed to keep her little guesthouse full and the creditors at bay, sometimes by the skin of her teeth.

> And now, thank God, some good news: my room with
> the sea view has been rented from July 3rd to August
> 15th. Now I've got three left. If those fill up, I'll just
> sleep up on the roof. Thank God it was just a warning
> about the gas bill. As long as there's life, there's hope.
> Our Dear Lord hasn't forgotten me!!! I do not feel anx-
> ious about anything and live day by day. (The dentist
> will kill me if I don't pay this month.)[26]

Rika worked and worked—determined to one day be able to offer her older children a prosperous, loving home, and determined to provide for her two Waldys, both the little one, who knew nothing of the complicated situation he had been born into, and the older one, who could have left her, but stayed.

4

Pension Walda

Crisis or no crisis, there was still something carefree about Scheveningen in the mid-1930s. Flags flapped in the wind over the beach clubs, the sky was clear, and the ocean breeze seemed to sweep all the gloominess and somber news stories out to sea. If there was one place where the exuberant twenties were still roaring on, it was in Scheveningen, still the most beautiful seaside resort town in the country. The art deco party hall at the end of the pier was one of the country's most popular stages for light entertainment, and night after night, it was jam-packed. The pier played host to major stars such as Willy Derby, Louis Davids, Duke Ellington, and the Andrews Sisters. And when the weather was nice, the boulevard was still buzzing with people. For no matter how dramatically people had to cut back, they still clung to a few sunny weeks of summer vacation by the sea—they simply had to spend them a bit more modestly than they used to.

Rika's business was booming. Her guesthouse may have been simple, but it was spotless, and her cooking could rival the expensive hotel cuisine. If at first guests were taken aback by the unorthodox constitution of the Nods family—which officially wasn't a family at all, since

Rika's last name was still technically Hagenaar and her son's was Van der Lans—their hearts were quickly melted by the household's warmth and charm. As a woman who clearly hadn't had it easy in life herself, Rika was someone people could trust with their troubles. She knew how to lift anyone's spirits, often taking out her tarot cards and astrology book and reading them with all the flair and conviction of a fortune-teller.

The host was an intriguing, exotic character, and his charming yet invariably proper company cheered up many a lonely lady. Perhaps this stemmed from the fact that he was at ease with the age difference between himself and the woman in his life. His son, little Waldy, was an exceptionally delightful boy with black curls and big blue eyes that observed the world around him with wonder. The guests watched tenderly as he "helped" his mother and her right-hand maid, Agnes, and brought the dinner plates to the table with an earnest look on his face. Page after page, the guest book was filled with thankful, sometimes almost lyrical messages about the "exceptional care" and "the tremendous warmth and hospitality" at Pension Nods.[27] "We almost don't want to leave," sighed one of the guests. Another left behind a poem of thanks:

> The sea is high, a storm's a churning,
> But by the beach the heat is burning.
> And when the temperature starts falling,
> Our charming hostess's house is calling.
>
> A house so homey, a house so gay,
> "Anjàs" will bring your dinner tray.
> At Pension Nods you'll dine with delight
> Oh, you'll surely find your appetite.
>
> And if you're feeling up for a little chat,
> You'll always have a place to hang your hat.

For a cup of tea and something sweet
Even little Waldy doesn't mind a treat.

Thank you, friends, for your hospitality
With this pen I shout out with glee
Long live the Nods family!
Yippee!

In April 1934, Rika rented two flats in a housing block that had just opened up on the Gevers Deynootweg, and the family moved again. The apartments were sunny and equipped with all the modern conveniences. They had parquet floors, leadlight windows, central heating, comfortable bathrooms, and even a refrigerator. They were a stone's throw away from the Kurhaus Hotel and only about twenty yards from the boulevard. Rika dubbed the new business Pension Walda, after the two men in her life, and herself. The smart-looking brochures she had printed emphasized the pension's "excellent Dutch cuisine" and—an essential selling point in those days—its "reasonable prices." As soon as she was sure that the guests wouldn't fail her that year either, the family moved into a third flat in the same housing block. From the top balcony she had a wide view of the backs of the luxury hotels and the fancy Sociëteit De Witte, and in between was a real glimpse of the North Sea.

From its very first season, Pension Walda was a smashing success. Known for its somewhat unconventional managers and easygoing atmosphere, the guesthouse became a favorite port of call for performers at the pier, which only made it more attractive to regular guests. Even soldiers on furlough from the Indies and German beachgoers came in large numbers to see "die liebe Leute van Walda"—the dear people of the Walda. Any guests who were drawn in by the establishment's somewhat German-sounding name weren't disappointed, for their host, who had recently obtained his degree in German mercantile correspondence, spoke the language flawlessly.

Holland's neighbors to the east—who just a few years earlier had been viewed as the great losers of Europe—were more than happy to be able to blow their extra German reichsmarks in Scheveningen again. As Holland and the rest of the Western world sank deeper into an economic depression, Germany was rapidly climbing out of one of its own. Everyone agreed that this miracle was largely thanks to the Austrian-born politician, Adolf Hitler, who, along with his henchmen on the Far Right, had noisily stepped into the spotlight at the end of the 1920s. At first, the established order had written him off as a shouting flash in the pan, but within a few years they were standing back and watching in wonder as he assumed absolute power. They say that suffering cleanses the soul, but, for both people and nations alike, this isn't always the case. The disillusioned masses of German voters found refuge in the National Socialist leader, who exuded the energy and vision they needed to pull their impoverished country out of its slump. And Hitler didn't disappoint. By the mid-1930s, inflation had stopped, unemployment was virtually nonexistent, and the German economy was running like a well-oiled machine.

Even Hitler's greatest political opponents were in awe of the man who had accomplished this incredible feat. Perhaps the Nazi ideas weren't as perilous as many people had feared. After all, weren't most of the concentration camps for political prisoners being shut down? And Jews and Communists were rarely being terrorized on the streets anymore, were they? Daily life had gone back to normal, and times were better than they had been in years. In Holland, many people hoped a Dutch Hitler would come along and save their economy, too, and in the 1935 elections at least 8 percent of voters cast their ballots for the NSB, the Dutch National Socialist Movement that had been established four years earlier by Anton Mussert. In The Hague and Scheveningen, that number was even higher at 12 percent.

But Rika didn't need a political party or a dictator to save her: she had created her very own *Wirtschaftswunder*, her own "economic miracle." Although she hadn't been raised to be anything but a house-wife, it turned out that she had inherited the Van der Lanses' flair for business. In the middle of a financial crisis, she somehow managed to turn her little guesthouse into a thriving operation. She had a flawless nose for new opportunities and an inexhaustible drive for getting things done. And, on top of that, she was fearless. When it became increasingly difficult for her landlord to find renters for his expensive apartments, Rika expanded her range of services. Pretty soon she was printing new brochures that read: "Walda Pension and Property Management Company: For the sale, rental, mortgage, insurance, administration and maintenance of homes."[28]

Rika continued to cook for her guests, but for the other work in the guesthouse, she relied on Agnes and four cheap Polish maids. In 1935, on the back of a photo for her children, she proudly wrote: "Mama with her employees!"

***

Even the Van der Lanses had to admit, their oldest daughter—the one who had seemed destined for total ruin just a few years earlier—was doing pretty darn well for herself. On the outside, Rika had always shrugged off the fact that she'd been banished from her family— "They're a crazy lot. In the end, I couldn't care less," as she wrote to Bertha after getting the cold shoulder at a birthday party—but deep down she was troubled by it, and in 1933, she started making frantic attempts at reconciliation.[29] "We simply aren't angels," she wrote in a letter to her parents on floral stationery. "We all have our good and evil qualities, and we all have our own cross to bear, we've all got our work cut out for us."[30]

Although Rika was never completely forgiven for all the shame she had brought to the family, and remained uninvited to birthday parties and New Year's celebrations, from then on, her relationship with her family gradually improved. Waldy frequently went to visit his grandparents—after all, it's not the little boy's fault, they reasoned. And especially the younger members of the family dropped by Rika's guest-house on a regular basis, where they always received a warm welcome—to them, the house even felt a little glamourous with all the artistic types coming and going. It was always a party at Rika's, or Aunt Riek's, and she never made a fuss about anything. If the place was a mess, she would simply say, "Who cares? Let's just sit with our backs to it, then we won't see it and it won't bother us." And as far as Waldemar was concerned, some members of the family never grew tired of mention-ing how he was "in fact"—in other words, despite his skin color—"a proper gentleman."

The only ones who couldn't enjoy the success and happiness at Pension Walda were Rika's own children, who were farther away than ever. In 1934, the Rijkswaterstaat had transferred Willem to a post in Groningen. Bertha, who had developed a strong bond with her friends in Goeree, had a particularly hard time moving up north. "We're a bit closer to The Hague now, but the trip from Groningen to The Hague costs fifteen gulden," she lamented in her diary. "We're even more iso-lated here than we were in Goeree."[31]

In the meantime, her parents' divorce had become final, and Bertha fervently hoped that her father would get married to Jans, their servant, who, under heavy protest, had left her own family and followed the Hagenaars to Groningen. Even though Willem continued to insist that Jans was their housekeeper, his children had figured out by then that there was more between the two of them than he let on. If they were to marry, Willem's situation would be more or less equal to that of Rika, thereby giving his daughter the moral freedom to rekindle a relation-ship with her mother. For even though Bertha hadn't seen her mother in years, she still missed her. One time, when she was staying with her grandparents in The Hague, she happened to pass by her mother's new guesthouse. Sadly, she wrote:

It was pitch black outside, but somehow my eyes
landed on Pension Walda. I didn't know exactly where
it was. Oh, how I wanted to go there. How happy she
would have been. We would have spent a wonderful
evening together. But before it even occurred to me
to get off the bus, we had already passed it. Tonight in
bed I'm going to go over the whole thing again in my
mind. Why do I still have to ride by my own mother?[32]

Willem showed no intention of marrying Jans, and he ruled his children's relationship with his ex-wife with an iron fist. They were strictly
forbidden to set foot in their mother's house before the age of twenty-
one, and that was final. And even though Bertha had already finished
school by then and had a job in an office, she still had enough respect
for her father's wrath to obey. Once, when she was in Scheveningen with
a friend and he suggested paying her mother a visit, she shrieked, "Oh
no, my father would never allow it!"

As for Rika, she stubbornly continued writing her weekly letters
and sending her children photos and little packages. She made no secret
of the fact that she was making good money. Bertha received a fur
coat and Henk, much to his delight, received a portable gramophone.
Dressed in her Sunday best, Rika would stand in the front yard of
Pension Walda and have photos taken with her employees, guests, son,
and other family members. The only person who was regularly absent
from the photos was Waldemar—no matter how provocative Rika was
wont to be, she was careful about putting her young lover on display.

In the meantime, Willem's once-magnificent career had reached a
dead end. The government could no longer afford costly public works
projects, and as a civil servant, he was increasingly subject to salary cuts.
The more Rika rubbed his nose in her good fortune and the closer his
children came to an age when they no longer had to follow their father's
orders, the more desperately Willem tried to hold on to his position of

power. The household battles raged on in Groningen, especially when
mail from The Hague arrived. And just as Wim had once tried to carry
glasses of water to his parents in the hope of calming them down, Bertha
was now the one trying to keep the explosive situation under control by
attempting to rein in her mother's impulsive behavior:

> In a week or so, I'll write to her again. The last letter
> wasn't so friendly, but that's because I can't tell Mama
> everything. I can't write and tell her that I'm longing
> for her so much these days. I'm afraid she will come
> here and say: I don't want my children to be upset.
> I can really imagine her doing something like that,
> which is why I have to write in a different tone.[33]

Finally, she decided to ask her mother to temporarily cut off contact
altogether.

> I just wrote a long letter to Mama. It will make her so
> happy. I also sent a photo and told her the truth, that
> she shouldn't write anymore. Maybe later things will
> be different.[34]

By the summer of 1935, the parental visitation arrangement was
back in effect, and Rika sent a short letter to Groningen once a year
to ask when she could see her children. The reply began with "Dear
Madam" and included nothing but a date, time, and location. On the
agreed-upon date, Willem brought his daughter and youngest son to
the train station in The Hague, where his ex-wife would be waiting for
them with little Waldy at the Hotel Terminus. She no longer dared to
take her children home with her, so they would go to Het Roomhuis,
a well-known restaurant in the Haagse Bos. But Rika wouldn't have
been Rika if she didn't give Willem a little wave from inside the taxi.

He would just stand there waiting at the tram stop, his face tight, trying in vain not to see the woman who had once been the love of his life.

For Henk, the annual visits to The Hague were fairly incomprehensible. He had only vague recollections of the mother he had been torn away from at the age of five, and to him, she was nothing but a strange, sweet-smelling woman who sent him nice presents and loving letters. While she and his sister were racing against the clock to catch up, Henk was left to play with little Waldy—a perfect stranger who just so happened to be his little brother and looked up at him with wide, expectant eyes. He understood little of what was happening, but early on he did try to get his sister to explain the situation to him:

> Yesterday Henk came and sat down beside me. It was
> just the two of us in the room. I told him there was a
> package from Mama. He said: Why don't we go there
> anymore, Sis? Did you know she came to Goeree?
> While we were swimming. She was wearing a pretty
> hat. Sis, I would like to go back and see her again. It's
> all so strange, Sis.
>   Now you can see he's picking up on things too.
> He only talks about it with me. I say: Papa and Mama
> don't like each other very much, and it's better this
> way. It's better for Mama and better for Papa too. But
> don't forget that you must always love Mama, Henk,
> because you have only one father and one mother.
> Then he crawled up onto my lap and wrapped his arms
> around me. I was quiet for a long time. Yes, Henk
> said, but they are angry at each other. Absolutely not,
> I said.[35]

In the meantime, Rika's two older sons, both stubborn Hagenaars, refused to have anything to do with their mother. When Wim and Jan ran into their mother and half brother by chance in Scheveningen in the summer of 1936, they looked away and acted as if they were invisible. Appalled, Bertha wrote: "Imagine that your own children, who you brought into the world, just walk past you. It's enough to make anybody crazy. I can really see it from Mama's perspective."[36]

But Rika refused to give up hope of being reunited someday. As pugnacious as ever, she wrote on the back of a photo of Waldy sent to Groningen: "If the boys only knew how much he loved them, they would regret every day that they just passed us by!!"[37] One day, the boys would break free from their father's iron grip and make their own choices, and perhaps then they would see that their mother's soul wasn't as black as they had been told all those years. And so, she kept up her provocative ways and continued sending loving letters and photos with captions such as: "Hello Sis, hello Henk, hello Jan, hello Wim, lots of love from Waldy," and "Remember your mom. I'm always with you! Mama."[38]

***

Just as Waldemar's ancestors had come from every corner of the globe, by the mid-1930s, their descendants had spread out in all directions. Hilda sent enthusiastic letters from the Dutch East Indies, where life was almost better than it had been in Suriname during the gold rush. And Waldemar's brother, Decy, was living in central Venezuela, where he had built his own power station. Occasionally, a letter would arrive in The Hague filled with his macho stories and photos of "Decy the tiger hunter." Lily, the beautiful baby of the family, had been sent sulking to Brazil by boat in 1930. The family figured that the only person who could handle the spoiled damsel was Koos Nods himself. Once there, she married a business associate of her father's and lived in the small city of Ouro Prêto, "Black Gold," where Koos had worked his way up to mayor and rode around on a donkey, inspecting the village.

He was now in his third marriage, this time to a German painter who ran his hotels.

Waldemar was still in Holland. Every morning he swerved through Scheveningen on his bicycle to his job in The Hague, always looking refined in his suit—perfectly tailored to his long, supple limbs—and his impeccably polished shoes; his eyes sparkled. He loved long bike rides in the fresh air, just as he loved long swims in the sea. As soon as the water was warm enough again, he would happily go back to being the tropical boy he once was. Every once in a while, he even felt at home in his new homeland, like the time a coal truck drove past him, and the driver, who was covered from head to toe in soot himself, shouted "Hey, blackie!" "Yeah? Look who's talking!" Waldemar yelled back in a gruff Hague accent. He came home grinning cheek to cheek—this was the kind of humor he had learned on the streets of Paramaribo. But on gray, wet days in the long months of winter, the luster would disappear from his skin and his eyes would grow dull. Whereas David Millar, who worked in the fast-paced world of aviation, seemed to have inherited Koos Nods's startling, almost aggressive charm, his introverted half brother was forced to spend his days in a gloomy bank in The Hague, where people were frantically clinging to their middle-class values in these perilous times.

The longer Waldemar lived in the Netherlands, the more he retreated into the role of the perfect gentleman, supremely civilized through and through, politer than polite, whiter than white. In Paramaribo, he could have glided through life as a son of a social elite, but here he was and remained "the token Negro," constantly having to justify his own existence. He had learned to turn a blind eye to the looks of Rika's sensation-loving friends and acquaintances and to ignore the condescension of his colleagues and superiors. Smiling, they sized him up with their eyes—but no matter how gentlemanly Mr. Nods looked and how conscientious he was in his work, he would always be a black man from that strange "monkey land" on the other side of the ocean. He

The Boy Between Worlds

couldn't find comfort or distraction in his work either, for in the current economic climate, career opportunities at mortgage lenders were virtually nonexistent. Many of his colleagues had already gone home to find the dreaded termination notice on their doorstep, so the fact that Waldemar still had his job was not to be taken lightly. The only thing he could do was continue his studies in the vague hope that he might someday get somewhere with them.

But in the meantime, he became serious and very quiet, old for his age, the candor of his early days in Holland all but lost. Waldemar missed the warmth and colors of *Switi Sranan*, the easygoing way of life in Suriname, where even people in the deepest poverty could still laugh and enjoy themselves. He missed the sun on his skin, and most of all, he missed the warm, languid river he'd loved so much. The only place he could still find the paradise of his youth was in the books that he and Rika read in their rare free time. The Sunday radio book hour was sacred: *Zuid-Zuid-West*, the nostalgic debut novel by fellow Surinamese expatriate Lodewijk Lichtveld, better known by his nom de plume, Albert Helman, was being read on the radio and was immensely popular.

> Now I am here in a strange city, and tomorrow I'll travel on, but where to? There is turmoil, or rather a small sense of sorrow that keeps pulling me farther and farther away, that leaves me constantly searching for something old, for something nearly forgotten.
>
> How could I have known back then, my poor Kutiri, that I would take that old sorrow and far-off longing with me to the city, to another country. How could I have known that the little house would be so beautiful under the coconut trees; how could I have known that the high rustle of the long palm leaves would sing even farther beyond the dull roar of the sea.

Zuid-Zuid-West calls to mind the dull, shimmering
day between the low coffee bushes. Oh, this country,
how could I ever forget this country![39]

The last contact that Waldemar had with his homeland were a few
letters exchanged with his late mother's family. The Treurniet family
faithfully sent their cousin packages with Surinamese spices and food
stuffs and kept him up to date on the latest news from the colony, which
hardly ever made it into the Dutch newspapers. That's how he first got
wind of Anton de Kom, a fellow ocean swimmer who had lost his job in
1932 and moved back to Paramaribo with his Dutch wife and children.
Upon his return, he started standing on the balcony of De Waag on the
Waterfront spreading Communist and nationalist views he had picked
up in the East Indian student circles of The Hague. Among Creoles,
who were still very loyal to Holland, his message fell on deaf ears, but
among the exploited Javanese contract laborers, he was garnering so
much support that, after a few bloody riots, the colonial government
promptly put him on a boat back to Amsterdam.

A few years later, Waldemar mourned with his family from a distance when the river that he loved so dearly took the life of one of his
cousins. The seventeen-year-old boy and his friends had been swept up
in a treacherous current that overturned their boat, and Waldemar's
cousin had disappeared into the deep without a trace. But his family
also sent him good news as well. His country was finally rising out of
the economic depression that had plagued the colony for decades. It
turned out that Suriname was rich in bauxite, the raw material used to
make aluminum, which was essential to the booming aviation industry. Foreign investment groups were gathering on the docks at the
Waterfront, and opportunities abounded for young European-educated
men like Waldemar Nods.

But even though Waldemar was the son of an adventurer and
born into a culture where men's fidelity was traditionally not of great

importance, he still didn't leave Rika. He responded stoically to the advances of girls on the beach who watched with pleasure as he emerged from the waves after a swim. Perhaps his Riek wasn't so young anymore or as beautiful as she had once been, but her arms were as warm as ever, and even in the face of all the misery around them, she was still quick to smile. She was his anchor in a cold world that never had been and never would be his own. In return, he was the silent force behind her bold attempts to fight back as a favorite daughter, mother, and respectable wife. They had both paid a high price for their love; maybe that's why they were so careful with it.

***

In the fall of 1936, little Waldy celebrated his seventh birthday. He was now in second grade at The Hague's first Montessori school. Before that, he had attended a preschool in Scheveningen, but the color of his skin and his illegitimate status had provoked so many comments that Rika had pulled him out of the school indignantly. The progressive, elite school in the south of The Hague was a far better fit for Waldy. There were many children with artistic parents, and the atmosphere was as free and playful as he was used to at home. Waldy had, as Rika once wrote, "a beautiful life with his father and mother."

Waldy was an exceptionally sunny little boy. For all he knew, life would always be as happy as it was then. His mother was always cheerful. She sang songs with him and turned every activity, from making beds to shopping in The Hague, into a fun, exciting adventure. He would ride in the tram with his nose pressed to the window, watching the wondrous world outside—the gas factory puffing out steam clouds, the giant mountains of coal piled up next to it, the crowds of people, and the cars honking in the street. And even though his mother was busy with her guests in the summer, one way or the other she always found time for him and held him in her arms any chance she'd get.

Waldy's father was his hero, and much more interesting than the other fathers. Not only did he look different and regularly receive exotic-smelling packages covered in colorful postage stamps from the mysterious world he came from, he also spent a lot more time with his son than other fathers did. Every spring, the two of them anxiously awaited the moment when they'd raise the flags on the public beach, signaling the opening of the season. From then on, they would spend every free moment together on the beach and in the water. When the weather was calm, they would swim out far from the coast, all the way to the lifeguard's raft where Waldy's father taught him how to dive with an elegant arch. Waldy always swam with his eyes wide open under water so he could see the fish and jellyfish.

When the fall came, and the flags were lowered, and the beach clubs dismantled for the winter, father and son would go for long walks through The Hague or to the movies. And in the early spring, as the sun was just regaining its strength and streaming into the windows in wide ribbons, the two of them would curl up like cats in the sun, and Waldemar would tell stories about Suriname, that faraway land where palm trees grew, and it was so warm you could swim every day. Waldy slowly began to understand that Scheveningen would never be his father's real home, no matter how good the three of them had it there. His home was on the other side of the vast ocean. On warm evenings, he would sometimes sit for hours and stare out at the sea with his dark green eyes, his homesickness almost palpable around him.

As Waldy got older, there were all kinds of uncles and aunts popping up in his life, all of whom found him interesting and wanted to take a photo with him. The same went for their houseguests, some of whom lived with them for years or kept coming back until they were almost like family. They pampered and spoiled him so much that even his mother complained. Waldy's favorite friend was the captain of the two Polish fishing vessels that docked in the Scheveningen Harbor. Sometimes he would pick Waldy up, hold him against his colossal belly, and buckle the belt of his uniform around him as if he were going to take him with him for the day. Waldy would roar with laughter, and the two would keep on tussling until his mother would have to come in, chuckling, to save him.

And then there were Waldy's older brothers and sister still living in Groningen. Once a week, a letter from his sister arrived, and his mother would rip it open with trembling fingers and flushed cheeks. She told the most wonderful stories about her other children, particularly Wim and Jan, his big brothers who couldn't come to visit him at the moment, she'd say, but someday they certainly would. His mother always beamed when she talked about "someday." And never had he seen her so nervous as she was once a year when they went with Bertha and Henk for tea at the café by The Hague zoo. His sister was just as nervous as his mother, but she always looked sweetly at him and stroked his curls. And even though his mother always encouraged him and Henk to play together, his brother never seemed to be in the mood and usually just sat there looking unhappy. To be honest, Waldy liked his brothers best in his mother's stories—they were like characters in a fairy tale, and as far as he was concerned, they could stay that way.

In December 1936, at the start of one of the coldest winters on record, Waldy went with his father to the movies in The Hague. That night he came down with a high fever. At first, his parents thought he was just a bit overexcited from the film, but the next morning, the little boy was unconscious and had to be rushed to the hospital. The doctors diagnosed an inflammation of the kidneys and lungs, and he spent the next several days on the brink of death. His parents kept watch at his bedside, their eyes filled with fear. Rika prayed for hours on end, promising over and over again to live a better life if Waldy pulled through. She was convinced that the vindictive God of her youth was punishing her for her pride and sins by threatening to take her youngest child from her too.

Waldy did pull through, and while he was recovering with months of bed rest and bowls of cream of endive soup, Rika set to work on her latest task: righting herself in the eyes of God. This was no easy feat. Her marriage to a Protestant had been followed by a divorce, and by living together out of wedlock with her non-churchgoing lover. In the eyes of the Roman Catholic Church, this was triple damnation at the very least. She hung crucifixes all over the house and set a giant statue of Mary on the fireplace mantel. From then on, Waldy spent his Sunday mornings with his mother at the Saint Anthony Abbot Church instead of playing outside like he had done before. He even had to have a first communion. He wasn't very impressed by the whole thing: the wafer nauseated him, and he was always getting reprimanded for not knowing his catechism.

It was on one of those Sunday mornings that his sunny view of the world first started to crack. He was sitting next to his mother on the hard church pew, wiggling his feet and hoping it would be over soon, when he suddenly heard a strange sound beside him. His mother was crying, and she couldn't stop.

***

On March 17, 1937, Rika and Waldemar married in The Hague city hall. The ceremony was exceptionally sober. It was so cold outside that the pier in Scheveningen was whitewashed in a layer of snow, and Waldy, who was still weak, had to stay home by the fire. There was hardly any family present, and the bride and groom were dressed in everyday clothes, though Rika couldn't resist sticking a few flowers from her bouquet in her hat. A few weeks later, Rika's letter arrived on the Wagenwegstraat in Paramaribo announcing their recent nuptials to her new Surinamese family. When they opened it, dried rose petals fluttered out of the envelope.

To his great disappointment, Waldy didn't return to the Montessori school that fall. From then on, he attended the Catholic school in Oud

Scheveningen. He missed his friends and had a hard time getting used to the working-class atmosphere and the church's strict approach to education. His classmates treated him like an ugly duckling, and one time, when he innocently told them about the summer he spent with his father on vacation in Lugano, Switzerland, because the doctor thought it would be good for his lungs, he was scolded for bragging. Who did he think he was, some kind of world traveler? For the first time in his life, he heard people comment on the color of his skin, calling him things like "nikker," "dirty brownie," or "ugly brown Chinaman." Waldy didn't understand—surely, he wasn't Chinese? And they certainly weren't dirty. In fact, he didn't know any man as clean as his father. Waldemar carefully rubbed his skin and hair with oil after every bath, ironed his shirts until there wasn't a wrinkle to be found, and constantly impressed on his son the importance of having a tidy appearance and perfect behavior, because "They're already watching us," he would say.

On his eighth birthday, Waldy was sent out to look in the shed behind their house, and inside a vegetable box he found a white fur ball staring back at him with deep black eyes. He had finally gotten the dog he had wanted for years—granted, "dog" was a rather generous word for the little Maltese pup his mother had been so thrilled about. The three of them decided to name the puppy Topsy, after a popular song that year, and because, as his mother declared, it went so well with Sonny Boy.

A few months later, on a bleak February day, there was another surprise for Waldy. His mother bundled him up in his warmest clothes, and he headed out with his father. The wind was blowing so hard that Waldemar had to hang on to him to keep him from being blown over. The wet streets around the boulevard were deserted, the sea was raging, and even the seagulls had taken shelter. The party hall at the end of the pier was nearly invisible behind the spurting clouds of foam. Wave after wave was crashing on the beach, and on the horizon, ships were fighting their way to safety in the Scheveningen Harbor.

Father and son plowed into the wind, passing by the chic hotels along the Seafront until they reached a beautiful villa, number 56. Waldy's father pulled a cluster of keys out of his pocket and said: "Look, this is our new house!" The long marble hallways seemed strangely quiet compared to the storm raging outside, and inside, the house was ice cold, having been vacant for nearly a year. Nevertheless, every detail attested to its prominence and grandeur. The house was very deep, and in the middle was a grand staircase that rose up to more than thirteen spacious guestrooms. In the back was a sheltered garden, and in the front was a large terrace on the first floor with a splendid view of the North Sea. To the left was the old village and harbor, and to the right the Kurhaus and the pier. It was an ideal location for the future home of Pension Walda.

There was a basalt slope directly in front of the house leading down to a parking lot where Waldy and his friends would later roller-skate between all the expensive cars. And on the other side of the parking lot was the beach, which was completely desolate at the moment, but in the summer would be teeming with beachgoers. "Just imagine, we'll be able to step out the door and into the sea!" his father said. Waldy saw the glimmer in his eyes and felt proud that they were going to live in such a beautiful house.

5

On the Seafront

The summer of 1938 was unprecedentedly hot. While the rest of the country was sweating under a massive heat wave, at the seaside it was glorious. The cool waves rolled peacefully onto the shore, and day after day, the sun climbed high in the sheer blue sky. In the evening, the sunbathers would lumber through the loose sand back to their temporary quarters with a feeling of deep satisfaction. At night, faint music and laughter drifted from the party hall across the smooth sea, and people sat out on the boulevard until the wee hours of the morning to enjoy the starry sky. For one last time, the seaside resort dazzled in all its nineteenth-century glory and grandeur.

Waldy spent the first weeks of his summer vacation in Goeree, where he stayed with his sister at one of her friend's places. Then—all dressed up like a little gentleman—he went to Switzerland with his father. His mother stayed home. She didn't like the mountains, she said, they obstructed her view. And what's more, in its first year at its new location at Seafront 56, Pension Walda was having the best season in its history. Rika combated her relentless longing for her oldest children and her remorse toward God in the only way she knew how: by staying busy. There was even a time when she slept in the bathroom because she had guests lodged in every nook and cranny of the house.

She wasn't the only one for whom 1938 was an excellent year. Germany's strongman, Adolf Hitler, was in his prime. As historian Sebastian Haffner would later write, if Hitler had died at the beginning of 1938, he would have surely gone down in history as a brilliant politician. The Germans could once again take pride in their country. Everything about Germany in the late 1930s was grand: the architecture, the masses cheering for their leader, and most of all, Hitler's ideas about the future—not just of Germany, but of the world. Inspired by his own misconception of Darwinism, he believed that people of the so-called Aryan race ought to fight each other until the strongest among them emerged and eventually took over the world. In Hitler's eyes, the German *Herrenvolk* under his leadership would undoubtedly come out on top.

Without a country of their own to call home, the Jewish people had spread out around the world and some assumed prominent positions. Hitler was convinced that they would sabotage the healthy competition he had envisioned. He claimed that they were responsible not only for Germany's humiliating loss in the Great War, but also for the economic crisis that had brought the country and the rest of the world to the brink of disaster. If Germany aimed to grow into the empire of Hitler's vision, it had to be completely cleansed of all Jewish stains. Although there was relatively little public violence against Jewish citizens in these years, a much more dangerous form of anti-Semitism was creeping into German society like a worm through an apple: on the outside everything looked shiny and healthy, but there was something much more sinister eating away at the core. Scores of legislative decisions made it virtually impossible for Jews to carry on with normal life, and those who could afford to do so sought refuge abroad, even if it meant handing over nearly everything they had to the German government.

Many wealthy German Jews immigrated to Holland, and by the end of the 1930s, there were seventeen thousand Jewish people living in The Hague, the second largest Jewish community in the country. A considerable majority settled in Scheveningen, which had been a haven for Jewish refugees for as long as anyone could remember. Rika was happy to support the businesses of the enterprising Jewish shopkeepers: she could relate to their resilience and flair for business. Waldemar, too, felt more at home with them than with the stiff Dutch, having grown up in Suriname, with its large population of Jews. In 1938, the Dutch National Socialist leader Anton Mussert even proposed deporting all European Jews to the colonies. Like much of the Surinamese Creole population, Waldemar probably had Jewish blood himself. When his grandmother Mietje got her freedom from Salomon Soesman in 1857 at the age of nineteen, she made use of the only capital she had: herself. No matter how black her son Koos's skin was, his features bore a striking resemblance to those of his mother's former master.

***

Having grown up on the Waterfront, Waldemar now lived on the Seafront. He and his family settled into the giant guesthouse suite in the fall of 1938, just as Scheveningen was preparing for its winter hibernation. He swam in the sea almost every day, its waters still warm from the summer sun, and Rika took countless happy photos of him in his bathrobe as he clambered down the basalt slope to the water. The two of them had had to fight for their love, but finally, it seemed as if their remarkable story, which had begun ten years earlier in the upstairs apartment on the Azaleastraat, was finally getting its happy ending.

But while Rika and Waldemar were busy writing their own story, world history was going rogue. Europe was in crisis, not just economically, but politically as well. In Spain, Franco and his Fascists were fighting a bloody civil war against the Left; in Italy, the Fascist dictator Benito Mussolini had seized power; and even in Greece, the cradle of democracy, an Extreme-Right leader was at the helm. And Adolf Hitler, the most extreme of them all, was becoming increasingly outspoken about the fact that a powerful and prosperous Germany was not enough; what he was really after was *Lebensraum*, or "living space" for his chosen people, a euphemism that justified the removal of anyone deemed racially inferior. From the moment he came to power, he began building a military force that was unparalleled in the world in scope and modernity. In early 1938, he pushed aside his generals, who, although loyal, were still too freethinking for his taste, and took the reins himself. That March, the German troops invaded Austria, making his own homeland officially part of the Greater Germanic Reich.

That fall, British Prime Minister Neville Chamberlain traveled to Munich to put a stop to the power-hungry German dictator's lust for war. "I believe it is peace in our time!" he announced triumphantly from the first floor of his official Downing Street residence, and even in the Netherlands, flags were raised in celebration of the fact that a second world war had been averted. But in the meantime, the British prime minister had given in to almost all of Hitler's demands, which had left Czechoslovakia virtually defenseless. On October 1, the German troops marched across the Czech border and took control.

Six weeks later, any illusion that perhaps the Nazis' anti-Semitism wasn't so bad after all was blown to smithereens. During the night of November 9, 1938, the windows of numerous Jewish shops and houses in Germany were smashed in. Owners were hunted down, robbed, abused, and in some cases, murdered. This event, called *Kristallnacht* after the shards of glass littering the shopping streets the next morning, sparked international outrage, particularly in Germany's neighboring countries, where there was growing concern about how easily Hitler was getting his way. In the spring of 1939, this concern became even more acute after he annexed Czechoslovakia to the Greater Germanic Reich without a struggle.

That summer, the artists and beachgoers showed up in Scheveningen as usual, and again Waldy went on vacation with his sister to Goeree and then with his father to Lugano. But all of Europe was holding its breath, and by the end of August, even the sunny seaside town had fallen under the shadow of Adolf Hitler. On August 31, a guest wrote in Pension Walda's guest book:

> We will look back on the wonderful sunny weeks we
> spent here at the beach in 1939 with great pleasure.
> What a pity that the international tension and decision
> to mobilize cast a shadow on the end of our holiday.
> May God turn it all into good.[40]

The next day, Hitler's army invaded Poland and left France and England with no choice but to declare war on Germany. Just twenty-one years after the end of the first Great War, a second one had broken out, and this time it was unlikely that the Netherlands could remain neutral. One needn't have been a military strategist to see that the Dutch coast was of great strategic importance for the power-hungry dictator to the east, and the small country's old-fashioned army was no match for the German military machine.

Waldemar and Rika were terrified. Jewish people weren't the only ones considered racially inferior in the Nazi philosophy. If this was how the Nazis were dealing with the Jews, what was their plan for people of color? The black race was even lower in Nazi eyes. In October, Waldemar's sister Hilda, and her husband, Jo Herdigein, came to stay on the Seafront. They were on furlough from the Indies and had already paid a visit to Koos Nods, who was still living in Ouro Prêto. To Waldy's delight, they brought him real leather soccer shoes and a hockey stick. For his father, they had a *pipiti*, a lump of real gold. It was the first time Waldy had ever seen photos of his mysterious grandfather: a gray-haired man with a proud posture and a weather-beaten face. Standing next to him was some kind of fairy princess—that must be his beautiful aunt Lily. One day, Waldy's mother pulled him aside and whispered a secret into his ear: maybe they, too, would be going to a warm country soon. Aunt Hilda didn't have any children herself, and she wanted nothing more than for her brother and his family to come live with them in the far-off Indies, far away from the threat of war that was now looming over Europe like a dark cloud.

Rika found herself in a nearly impossible situation. Although she would have loved to have seen her two Waldys safe and happy, and although she would have loved to embark on an adventure to the colonies herself, leaving for the Indies would force her not only to give up her marvelous guesthouse, but also to say goodbye to her four oldest children all over again, most likely forever, and just as they were starting to feel within reach. Earlier that fall, Bertha had invited her to come to Groningen and spend a few days getting to know her future husband. While she was there, something remarkable happened: Wim decided he wanted to take advantage of the occasion to introduce his fiancée to his mother. And so, after ten years, Rika saw her oldest son again. The confused, angry little boy had grown into a tall, disciplined young man. During their visit, he was exceptionally cold toward his mother. But no matter how short and formal their meeting had been, Rika was convinced that this was a new beginning, if only because Wim's fiancée struck her as a warmhearted woman who wouldn't dare to keep her future children away from their grandmother.

Naturally, Willem Hagenaar was livid when he heard that his ex-wife had visited his children in Groningen. He was so angry that he even threatened to kick his daughter out of the house once and for all. Bertha wrote:

> I still need to write about Mama's visit to Groningen
> in September. She stayed at Hofman's, and the days
> we spent together were unforgettable. I am happy that

> Johan was able to get to know her. But what a com-
> motion it created. I almost ended up in Scheveningen.
> I felt so much motherly love in those few days, and so
> did Henk. He writes to Mama much more often now.
> Things are really shaping up between us. And once we
> have our own house, I hope we get to see for ourselves
> that life can be different.[41]

Willem's outburst, however, was the final fit of rage in a battle that had already been lost, for it now seemed that no amount of threats could stop the relationship between twenty-two-year-old Bertha and her mother. Soon after, Bertha spent her first night at Pension Walda, and the two, mother and daughter, later traveled together to Goeree for the wedding of one of Bertha's friends. "Everyone found it perfectly normal that Mama and I were together," Bertha wrote, both surprised and elated.[42] In 1939, mother and daughter spent Christmas together for the first time in nine years.

Shortly before that, the Nods family had bid Aunt Hilda and Uncle Jo farewell on the Rotterdam quay with a heartfelt "See you soon!" In the end, Rika had decided to put the safety of her husband and son first, and Uncle Jo had promised to do everything he could to find a suitable job for his brother-in-law as quickly as possible. Meanwhile, Rika did what she could to make up for the lost years and showered Bertha with her motherly love and advice. Under no circumstances was her daughter to make the same mistakes she had made:

> You aren't the only victim of your parents' divorce, my
> dear. Therefore, Sis, I *really* want to make sure that
> you do not take marriage too lightly. Sweetheart, don't
> get married *to be free*. Because that is what you won't
> be. If you marry, you will *not* be free. You'll just think
> you are! And that's precisely when you are bound.

But . . . it should be a bond so full of love, trust, and
sacrifice that you never feel it. If you really take that to
heart, everything will be alright. You are two different
people. And you should never demand too much of
each other. One's nature is one's nature. Adapt to each
other—and to each other's shortcomings as well.

Always share everything with honesty and love.
And if you know you want something that the other
doesn't, don't force it! That which is freely given is so
beautiful and so sacred! Honestly, my sweet children,
there is no reason to rush into marriage. First focus on
the foundation of the marriage. Never deprive yourself
of freedom. I beg you, Sis, *never* do that; I worry about
that sometimes. That should *never* ever happen. You
are only young once. Enjoy it. Once you're married,
you'll be burdened with heavy responsibilities; the rent
will have to be paid, the taxes will have to be paid, the
gas and electricity bills will have to be paid, you will
need furniture, food, bread, meat, etc. You'll have to
be able to pay for the doctor; you'll need life insurance.
Children will be born, and they will need care. You
have seen misery. Motherly love alone is not enough.
Life is hard, it *requires money*.[43]

In her heart of hearts, Rika wasn't particularly impressed with
Bertha's fiancé, who seemed neither intellectually nor temperamentally
fit for her high-strung daughter. When the Dutch army was mobilized
in February 1940 and Pension Walda provided quarters to two soldiers,
Rika sought every opportunity to bring Bertha into contact with the
strapping, intelligent young men staying in the house. No expense or
effort was spared to make the defenders of the fatherland feel at home,

and when her daughter was visiting, bottles of wine were hauled out of the cellar, and the evening would inevitably turn into a lively party.

For ten-year-old Waldy, it was a wonderful period. Real soldiers were staying in his house! He could hardly imagine anything more exciting than the old helmet they gave him. It was displayed in a place of honor, right next to his leather football shoes. He was growing quickly—"already a real kid," as his mother wrote to Henk with pride—and he was allowed to stay up increasingly late during the long, convivial evenings at Pension Walda, even though his father grumbled about it sometimes.[44] If Waldy ever wanted to be a doctor—something his parents ardently hoped—then he had to make sure he did his homework. For although he had managed to adjust to the strict Catholic regime, his love for school hadn't exactly grown over the years. There were so many other more interesting adventures for a boy of his age, like roller-skating in the parking lot on the boulevard, catching shrimp and fishing for plaice off the pier, and waging mothball wars between mattresses in one of the big hotels managed by his best friend's father.

May 5, 1940, was a particularly golden day at Pension Walda. Not only because Bertha was there, but because it was one of the first truly warm days of the year. The soldiers brought home ice cream, which the houseguests enjoyed in the garden behind the house on the Seafront. Happily, they all posed for Waldemar's camera around the wooden garden bench—the soldiers, the Nods family, and the Polish servant girls who had returned to Scheveningen for the summer rush. Topsy frolicked around in the background, still very much the happy puppy. However, the captions Rika wrote on the back of the photos in the days that followed were notably less sunny: "Frightening times, May 1940."

The next Friday, May 10, Waldy woke up to the sound of the radio. Downstairs he found his father already completely dressed. The radio announcer's loud, agitated voice filled the room: that morning, at the break of dawn, five minutes before four, a fleet of hundreds of enemy planes had crossed the eastern border into the country. At that very moment, seaplanes were landing on the New Meuse River in Rotterdam, and thousands of German paratroopers were floating to the ground around the airports. There was a tremendous amount of enemy activity in The Hague, evidently with the objective of taking the government and royal family captive. "Are they going to shoot here, too, Dad?" Waldy asked. "I don't think so," his father replied, "but you never know." The words had barely rolled off his tongue before a black plane thundered right over their house and the roar of rattling machine guns broke out on the boulevard.

A few minutes later, when Waldy and his father carefully climbed upstairs and peeked out the window, they saw three seaplanes in the surf in front of their house. Just then, a large, expensive automobile stopped on the Seafront. A passenger stepped out hastily and hauled two suitcases out of the car. As the car drove away, he scrambled down the stone slope, carrying one of the suitcases, and ran across the parking lot toward the beach. One of the pilots ran up to meet him, hoisted him up on his shoulders, and dragged him through the surf to the plane. Shortly afterward, the aircraft taxied out and took off toward England. Waldy's father had recognized the refugee: it was Eelco van Kleffens, the new Dutch minister of Foreign Affairs. As the plane disappeared on the horizon, the deafening shooting broke out again. German fighter jets swooped down like black shadows, and the two other seaplanes went up in flames. Huddled behind the window, Waldy and his father could hear the pilots screaming as they burned alive. Standing in front of their house was a single lonely suitcase, left behind by the runaway minister.

May 10, 1940
Friday morning, 9:00

> Dear children!
> Couldn't get the package out, we're at war. May
> God protect you all, and may you come to your Mother

if you can. There is room here, the sea is calming. Two
poor pilots were shelled before our very eyes, pray to
Mary, stay in good spirits. May God bless and protect
all of you. I can't write anymore, received your letter
today. Stay calm, Mother is praying for all of you, lots
of love and hugs from your Mother and the Waldys.[45]

That day, the Polish captain fled the Scheveningen Harbor with
his fishing vessels. Waldy spent the day helping his father build a
bomb shelter out of sandbags behind their house, while his mother
started stocking up on emergency supplies. The next morning, the radio
announced that the Dutch army had put up a courageous fight and shot
down hundreds of German planes. Everyone in the guesthouse cheered.
But that Sunday, Crown Princess Juliana fled with her husband and
two daughters to England, and Queen Wilhelmina followed the next
day, along with the last remaining members of the Dutch government.

On Tuesday afternoon at 1:25, a fleet of Heinkel bombers appeared
over Rotterdam like thick black hornets against the blue sky, and ten
minutes later, they flew back to the east, leaving behind seven hundred
dead, thousands wounded, and a giant sea of flames where the bustling
city center had stood that morning. From their back balcony, Waldy
and his mother could see the black clouds above Rotterdam and the
Pernis oil towers. The next morning, May 15, they cried together as the
radio announcer reported that the commander in chief of the Dutch
military, Henri Winkelman, had surrendered after the Germans had
threatened to bomb Utrecht as well. But Rika was quick to dry her
tears: crying doesn't get you anywhere, she said, and it was only a matter of time before the British warships would appear on the horizon to
set them free.

The next day, the soldiers at Pension Walda were demobilized.
Upon leaving, one of them wrote in the guest book:

A half-year of mobilization and four days of war have
brought us as close together as many years of friendship. It was during the fearful time around May 10th
that our faith in the Netherlands was strengthened by
the residents of Pension Walda.[46]

As abruptly as the war broke out, life slid back to normal. While
beachgoers became fewer and farther between and Rika was busy trying
to save her summer season, the new regime was setting up its headquarters under the leadership of Reich Commissioner Arthur Seyss-Inquart
on the Clingendael estate near Scheveningen. In June, a unit of the
Waffen-SS would be stationed in the seaside town to guard the harbors
and lighthouses. On the boulevard, a German brass band played happy
tunes and high-ranking soldiers in sweltering leather jackets posed for
photos beside the donkeys on the beach: See, life under the new order
isn't so bad. Pension Walda housed German soldiers as well. The men
were bored to death, and it wasn't long before family acquaintances were
earning a bit of extra money playing cards with them on the Seafront.

With the same pragmatic business spirit that led the Dutch into
the slave trade in the seventeenth century, they adapted to life under
the Nazi regime. It seemed as if there was little else to be done; Hitler's
war machine was plowing across the Continent like a tank, seizing one
country after another. On May 28, Belgium surrendered, followed by
Norway on June 9. And on June 22, Hitler won his sweetest victory of
all: France, the country that had so humiliatingly brought Germany to
its knees in 1918. By the end of the summer, most of the Continent was
under German rule. Only England, protected by the same waters that
the Nods family could see from their house, was still resisting, but it
seemed only a matter of time before the British Isles would be annexed
to the Greater Germanic Reich as well, for, as Hitler declared in a radio
address: "I am a man who has only known one thing: to conquer, conquer, and conquer again."

At Pension Walda, the occupiers and guests were living peacefully together for the time being. Rika had a big heart and had encountered too many kind and polite Germans in the years leading up to the war to assume that there was a devout Nazi hiding under every steel helmet. Leaving for the Indies was no longer an option—all sea connections between the colonies had been cut off in May 1940—and expressions of gratitude continued to fill the pages of Rika's guest book. One guest wrote:

> What better way for an officer's wife whose husband
> has been taken captive to spend her vacation with two
> little toddlers than at Pension Walda, where a cheerful
> atmosphere prevails, and the food is outstanding—
> even under rationing.[47]

Bertha had followed her mother's advice and come to The Hague. She worked for the fire inspector and visited the Seafront on an almost daily basis. Rika now addressed her weekly letters to her son Henk, who was sixteen by then and still living with his father in Groningen. He wrote back to her regularly—but not without plenty of encouragement on her part.

> My dear Henk,
>   Now that you've done your best to write a nice
> long letter, I truly know you are my great, brave son.
> Because, my dear boy, believe it or not, every breath I
> take is for my sweet children. My spirit is always with
> you, my heart is always with my darling children. And
> if all I get are a few sober, hastily written scribbles, I
> grit my teeth and think, oh how a mother can feel so
> poor.

Consider it your duty now, you hear? I won't be
the least bit angry if you don't have time for a long letter. But I need to hear something from you every week.
And you know, Henk, it makes me so happy.[48]

In her letters to Henk, Rika often wrote about memories from a
time when they were all together ("I still remember how you all decorated my chair") or went on and on about the daily adventures of his
little brother Waldy ("He is crazy about his father. They're sitting here
like two little boys making plans for the vacation") or replied to Henk's
news ("I think it's wonderful that you are learning to dance so well.
Your mother has always been number one in that department").[49] At
the same time, she tried to tell her son what she hadn't been able to for
all those years: her side of the story.

What happened between your Mother and your Father
is something you can't possibly understand, my dear.
Later, when you're a grown man, your eyes will be
opened. And, my dear boy, you will be happy that you
always stayed true to your dear sister and mother.
God only knows that the one thing driving me
was the thought of your futures, for which I was willing to hand over my greatest treasures on earth to their
father. Unfortunately . . . this choice has been scandal-
ously abused to present my dear children with a very
different story of what happened. But God will hold us
all accountable, and He alone knows how much I have
done for my children and that my heart was weaker
than my reason. For I never should have done it. God
never forsakes those who trust in Him.[50]

Although Henk had no idea what he was supposed to do with these kinds of emotional outpourings from a woman he had seen all of ten times since he was a toddler, he was kindhearted and friendly by nature and crazy about his sister. And now that she lived in The Hague and was one of the family at his mother's house, going to the Seafront no longer seemed like such a big step, especially now that his father seemed to have more or less given up the fight against it. In 1940, he visited his mother at her house for the first time. Giddy with happiness, Rika ushered him into the attic room with a sea view, which had been outfitted with every convenience. "This is your room now," she said, even though Henk knew full well that there would be beach guests staying there in the summer. She also told him his fortune. "One day, you will be an architect, and you'll come pick your mother up in a car," she predicted.

From that point on, Henk came to the Seafront on a fairly regular basis, usually accompanied by a cousin. He was finally able to get to know the man who had been such a thorn in his father's side and who had always been referred to by the Hagenaar children as "the old Waldy," to distinguish him from little Waldy. He really liked him. He wouldn't discover until much later how wide the age gap between his mother and her elegant second husband was or what a huge scandal their love for each other had created.

While Henk may have still been uneasy about his new relationship with his mother, Rika picked up the thread as if she had had him at her side all those years. Proudly, she wrote to Bertha:

> Henk looks so handsome, I think he has gotten more good-looking. He had a delicious dinner with us and stayed around for tea. His cousin wasn't with him, which I rather liked. You just want to be alone sometimes, you know, Sis? My children are so different, and I mean that honestly! His friend is a nice boy, but there is something so different about him. Henk is a real,

respectable dear, I'm proud of him. I hope he comes
back soon.[51]

At the dawn of 1941, the Netherlands was under occupation, but
life had never been better for Rika and Waldemar. That fall, a fat letter
arrived from Groningen. It was from Jan, the son Rika hadn't heard
from since 1929, when he left as an eight-year-old boy, following his
big brother's lead. Rika had faithfully sent him letters and presents for
years and relentlessly tried to get in touch with him via her other children: "Give Jan a secret kiss for me and after you've done it, tell him it
was from his mother!!" and "Show this photo of Waldy as a boy scout
to Jan, and tell him that he never needs to be embarrassed of his sweet
little brother."[52] And time and again, she wrote: "Bertha, write me lots
about the boys, it makes me so happy."

Not once had Jan acknowledged that his mother still existed. But
he had recently been thrown out of the house by his father because
not only had he grossly neglected his studies, but he also had a secret
relationship with a girl who was Catholic, like his mother. Ever since
his disastrous marriage had come to an end, Willem had become even
more devoutly anti-Catholic than his father was, and the thought of his
son converting to Catholicism was too much for him to swallow. As Jan
wrote in a letter to an uncle:

> I've written to Father many times, but his answer was
> always so disappointing that it has reached a point that
> I have finally accepted our new relationship. I don't
> think things will ever be right with him again. His hate
> for all things Catholic runs too deep for him to make
> an objective judgment.[53]

Laughter was something Rika had always been capable of, but sel-
dom had she looked so delighted as the first time she posed in front of

her husband's camera with her now quite grown-up son. Despite their long separation, it turned out that they still got on marvelously with each other. Like his mother, Jan was a happy rascal full of stories and an urge for adventure. His uncles, who had followed in father Van der Lans's footsteps and gone into the fruit and vegetable business, went to great lengths to help him get his life back in order. Uncle Marcel arranged a job for him, and as far as his religious education was concerned, Uncle Jan found a priest who was willing to help his namesake make up for lost time. When it turned out that work and school weren't a good combination, the two uncles created a sort of scholarship fund so that he could study economics at the Rotterdam University of Applied Sciences.

Due to the rationing of basic commodities, Christmas dinner 1941 was a frugal affair compared to the feasts served at Pension Walda in the past. But for Rika, it was a sumptuous evening, because she found herself surrounded by three of her five children. In addition to Waldy and Bertha, Jan was there with his fiancée. At church, Rika fervently thanked the Lord for "the great joy of having my boy back in my life."[54]

Waldy was deeply impressed by his jovial big brother. He had heard heroic stories about him throughout his entire childhood, and now he had suddenly materialized:

> He mimics everything Jan does. Sometimes Waldemar
> says, that's enough, talk normally! I'll tell you, my
> children are absolutely destined for the theater. The
> best one is Sis—it's scandalous, but it always makes me
> laugh so hard. And Waldemar really means it, because
> the little rascal knows I can't help but laugh, and it's
> not good parenting for Ma to laugh at something Pa
> has forbidden.[55]

The only one who remained steadfast in his rejection of his mother was Wim. He had gotten married and taken over a family medical practice in a small village in Friesland. Jan tried to mediate, but:

> Wim irrevocably cut ties with Mama at a certain
> age, and deep-down he is absolutely convinced
> that there never was and never will be another way.
> Consequently, he has kept his distance from the Van
> der Lans family as well. Wim is fully aware that his
> position is disputable, but he is someone who never
> does things halfway.[56]

For once, micro and macro history seemed to be perfectly aligned. Christmas 1941 wasn't only a joyful turning point for Rika, but for the war as well. When Hitler gave the green light the previous summer for Operation Barbarossa, the great campaign against Russia, he was so sure that the Soviet Union would prove as easily conquerable as Europe that he didn't bother to outfit his troops for the winter. But the Russians successfully deployed the scorched-earth policy, retreating farther and farther inland and burning everything in their wake. This forced the German armies to spread out across a wide area, creating problems with their supplies. Once the fierce Russian winter set in, the Germans finally met their match, and in early December 1941, the invincible Hitler lost his first major battle in Moscow.

Had the German leader been a full-blooded politician, he could have chosen to consolidate his position and offer his people—who had followed him with doglike devotion into his wars—a period of peace. But Hitler's desire to conquer was so overpowering that he could not stop at defeat. Being denied his Russian victory seemed to spoil the game for him, and from that point on he was after total Armageddon. The first victim would be the country he had specifically chosen for his empire, which had then dared to disappoint him. On November 27, he announced in a radio address: "If the German people are no longer strong enough and prepared to sacrifice their blood for their existence, then they shall pass away and be destroyed by another, stronger power . . . and then I will not weep for the German people."

In the early morning of December 7, 1941, Germany's most important ally, Japan, bombed the American war fleet anchored in Pearl Harbor. The attack was as surprising as it was destructive. America declared war on Japan, Hitler declared war on America, and by then there was hardly any part of the world that wasn't involved in the European war. Curaçao and Suriname were occupied by American troops to safeguard the raw materials so precious to the war industry. As Prime Minister Gerbrandy, leader of the Dutch government in exile in London, predicted: "This war will be won with waves of oil and shipments of bauxite."

Waldemar's final ties to his homeland had now been severed, and when the Japanese invaded the Dutch East Indies in 1942, his contact with his sister was cut off abruptly. Every evening, he listened tensely to the news from the front on English radio, hoping to hear that the Allies had invaded Europe, the continent that couldn't hold out much longer. But Berlin was well aware of the vulnerability that the western coast of the Nazi empire presented; thus, the order was given to build an over sixteen-hundred-mile-long line of defense along the North Sea coast— the Atlantic Wall. Two major bases were soon to be established in the Netherlands: one in IJmuiden and the other in Scheveningen. And a thick line was drawn down the topographic map, straight through Pension Walda.

Rika and Waldemar hardly noticed anything at first, though more and more German observation posts were cropping up on the boulevard, beach, pier, and the roofs of the major hotels. The number of bookings for the coming summer season dropped dramatically, and money became so tight that Rika was forced to sell a portion of her furniture in March and borrow from one of her brothers. "I am a victim of the war," she wrote to him apologetically and promised he would get his money back as soon as the warm weather returned and the first beachgoers showed up on her doorstep.[57] In early April, however, the occupiers declared both the beach and the dunes off-limits. This was a death sentence for both Scheveningen and the guesthouse alike.

If Rika and Waldemar had hoped to be able to stay on the Seafront regardless, their hopes were shattered one month later. The mayor of The Hague ordered that 309 houses in strategic locations be vacated; a police officer arrived at number 56 to deliver the terrible news. The Nods family was summoned to hand over their house keys at police headquarters by May 22, and in exchange, they were assigned a temporary residence in Rijswijk. In a few weeks full of confusion and haste, Pension Walda disappeared, and with it everything that Rika and Waldemar had put so much love and effort into building over the years. "Here in Scheveningen, everyone is packing their bags. Mama is already lugging around big suitcases," wrote Jan, who was living with his mother at the time.[58] Waldemar took one last photo of his son on the beach, standing at the edge of the surf in a jacket a bit too large for him. It was an unusually chilly and overcast spring day, and the round pavilion at the end of the pier behind him looks like a sea palace in the mist. Just as the first inscription in Rika's guest book had been written in German, so was the last. It came from one of their military guests, who, after having felt so welcome in their home, was forced to move on. "I felt at home here with the Nods family," he wrote. "Too bad I have to go. Duty calls."[59]

(L–R) Eugenie, Lily, Waldemar, and Hilda Nods, Paramaribo, 1921.

The Waterfront in Paramaribo, 1920. Tropenmuseum Collection, Amsterdam, coll.or. 0-410.

The warehouses of the Royal Dutch Steamboat Company in the port of Paramaribo.
Tropenmuseum Collection, Amsterdam, coll.no. 60006866.

The SS Oranje Nassau *in front of the Surinamekade in Amsterdam.*
National Maritime Museum Collection, Amsterdam.

Rika van der Lans on the occasion of her first holy communion, 1903.

The Van der Lans children circa 1911.
(L–R) Jo, Bob, Rika, Marie, Bertha, Mien, Jan, and Marcel.

Rika at the age of seventeen, 1908.

The Hagenaar family, Den Bosch, 1922.
(L–R) William, Wim, Bertha ("Sis"), Jan, and Rika.

A Surinamese man in Goeree, 1927. On the motorcycle, from left to right: Bertha, Jan, Willem, and Wim. Seated, from left to right: David Millar next to an unknown man and Rika with baby Henk.

Rika with her children, December 1928.
(L–R): Bertha, Henk, Rika, Jan, and Willem.

Waldemar and Rika on the Azaleastraat in The Hague, January 1929.

Waldemar (second row, third from left) with handball team, April 12, 1929.

Waldemar on camping trip with Wim, summer 1929.

Waldemar on camping trip with Wim, summer 1929.

Waldemar and Rika on the beach with Bob and friend, 1929.

Rika on the beach.

Waldemar swimming in the Zuiderpark, The Hague, summer 1929.

Waldemar kayaking with a friend.

*Rika and Waldemar,
The Hague, 1929.*

Rika with the newborn Waldy, The Hague, December 1929.

Apprentice accountant Waldemar, 1931.

Waldemar with colleagues.

"Sonny Boy."

"Sonny Boy."

Waldemar's brother Decy in the
jungle: "Sending warm greetings."

Hilda Nods, Holland, November 1931.

The young Nods family, summer 1932.

Rika and Waldy, The Hague in 1933.

Waldy, spring 1933.

Bertha and Henk's last visit with their mother for a while, summer 1933.

Father and son on the beach in Scheveningen, circa 1933.

Father and son at the beach in Scheveningen, circa 1933.

Waldy at the beach in Scheveningen, circa 1933.

The two Waldys at the beach in Scheveningen, circa 1933.

Waldy at the beach in Scheveningen, circa 1933.

Waldy and a friend.

Pension Walda on the Gevers Deynootweg.

Pension Walda on the Gevers Deynootweg.

Pension Walda on the Gevers Deynootweg.

Pension Walda, 1933.

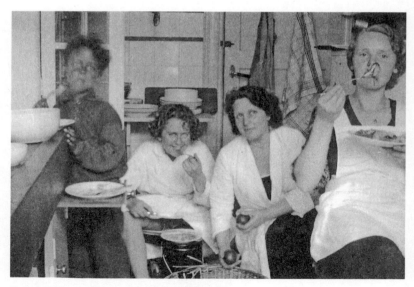

Pension Walda, 1933: "Mama with her employees!"

Rika and Agnes, 1933.

After a swim: Rika with her two Waldys on the balcony. Scheveningen, 1934.

*Rika with her mother
in front of Pension Walda,
Gevers Deynootweg.*

*Rika briefly reunited with son
Henk and daughter Bertha.
Seated: Waldy and Henk. Het
Roomhuis in The Hague, 1935.*

Rika with her flourishing family during a time of crisis. Scheveningen, 1936.

Waldy with Topsy.

Waldy with a new scooter.

Waldy and his father.

Waldy with a rabbit, 1937.

*With Topsy on the Seafront.
Scheveningen, circa the late 1930s.*

Climbing up from the beach to the guesthouse on the Seafront.

Rika with sister Jo, in the living room on the Seafront.

The Zeekant, seen from the boulevard. The Hague Municipal Archives Collection.

At the Pension Walda on the Seafront. (L–R) Waldy, Waldemar, Rika, Bertha, and Topsy.

With guests at Pension Walda.

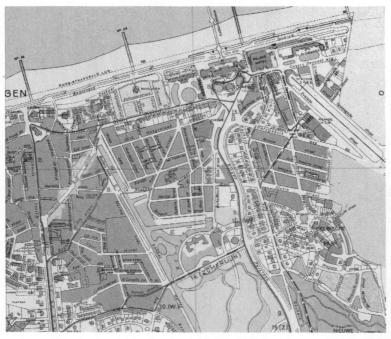

Map of The Hague, 1938. The Hague Municipal Archives Collection.

Bertha and Topsy, with the party hall on the Scheveningen pier in the background.

Waldemar on holiday.

Christmas 1939.

On the eve of the war, spring 1940.

On the eve of the war, spring 1940.

On the eve of the war, spring 1940.

Bertha, Topsy, and Rika, Scheveningen, 1941.

Rika, 1942.

Waldy (center, first on the left), "Quick Steps" Catholic soccer club, The Hague, 1941.

Jan, Rika, and Bertha, September 1942.

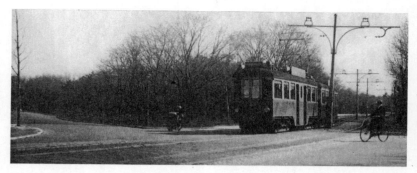

The Blue Tram on the way to the Gevers Deynootweg. The Hague Municipal Archives Collection.

Waldy and Rika, September 29, 1943.

In preparation for a possible Allied attack, the Germans ordered the pier to be burned in 1943. NIOD Collection.

Betty Springer.

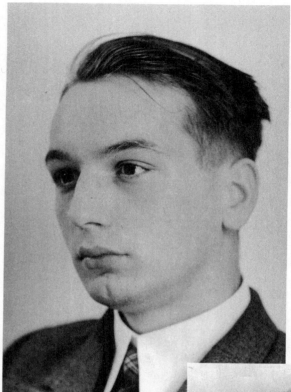

Resistance hero Kees Chardon, "the little lawyer."

Jew hunter Kees Kaptein, "the greatest Jew crusher in the Netherlands." National Archives, The Hague.

Sign of life from Rika, tossed from the train on the way to the Vught concentration camp, May 10, 1944.

The gates of Neuengamme, where the post office was likely located.

The gates of Neuengamme, where the post office was likely located.

The Cap Arcona *in its glory days.*

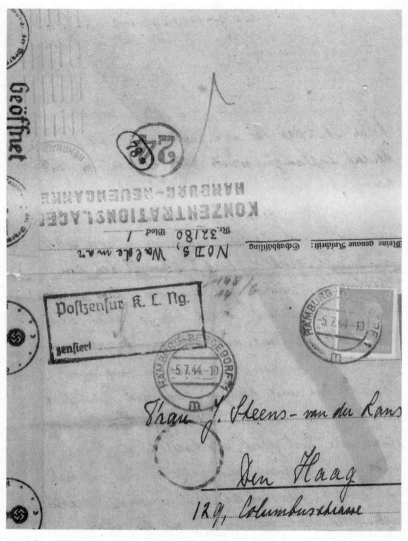

Letter from Waldemar Nods from the Neuengamme concentration camp, block 1, July 2, 1944.

Liebe Jo, dass Du von mir einen Brief in
Deutsch empfangen würde, das hast Du nie denken
können. Für mich war es auch eine grosse Über-
raschung. Wie geht es die allen, deine Eltern,
und Rich und Waldie mein Jungen wie geht's
dir. Mir geht's gut, obwohl ich am
liebsten in Holland geblieben wäre, das wird
Du doch verstehen. Es ist hier ja alles ganz
anders wie bei uns, und ich muss wieder von
vorne herein anfangen. Willst du mich mein
Rasierapparat, mit Klingen, Seife und Rasierpinsel
schicken und ein paar Strümpfe. Hast Du noch
etwas von Rich gehört, ich hatte sie in Holland
einige Briefe geschrieben und hatte die bestimmt auch
mal gesehen. Schreibst du bald wieder und Waldie
auch. Viele herzliche Grüsse an die allen
Waldie.

Letter from Waldemar Nods from the Neuengamme concentration camp, block 1, July 2, 1944.

Map of the Bay of Lübeck, with X indicating where the sinking of the
Cap Arcona *occurred. Hannie Pijnappels.*

The Cap Arcona *on fire, Bay
of Lübeck, May 3, 1945.
Neuengamme photo archive.*

Marcel van der Lans's ad in the newspaper, June 1945.

Rika's prayer card.

Grootere liefde heeft niemand dan hij, die zijn leven geeft voor zijn vrienden.

Joh. XV, 13

Rika's prayer card.

✝

Bid voor de Ziel van
Mevrouw
HENDRIKA NODS-
v. d. LANS,

geboren 29 September 1891 te 's-Gravenhage en
overleden plm. Februari 1945 in het Concentratie-
kamp Ravensbrück.

═══════

Heb medelijden met mij, o God, overeenkomstig
Uwe groote barmhartigheid.   Psalm 50, 3.

Ik zal opstaan en tot mijnen Vader gaan en
Hem zeggen: Vader, ik heb gezondigd tegen den
hemel en tegen U. Ik ben niet waardig Uw
kind genoemd te worden.

Maar de Vader zeide: Laten wij blijde feest-
maal houden want dit, mijn kind, was dood
voor mij en het is herleefd. Het was verloren
en is teruggevonden.   Lucas 15, 18.

Wie uwer zonder zonde is, werpe den eersten
steen op haar.   Joh. 8, 7.

Veroordeelt niet en gij zult niet veroordeeld
worden.   Lucas 6, 37.

Onze Vader. — Wees Gegroet.

R. I. P.

A. N. Govers N.V. - Den Haag

Waldy in uniform: "A scout whistles
under all circumstances."

Waldy in the last year of war, Hoogkarspel.

Waldy (top row, first from the left) with his school team, 1950.

Waldy on the shore, spring 1942.

Statuette of Sonny Boy in the library in Scheveningen, made by Teus van den Berg-Been.

6

Life in the Shadows

As sad as Rika was about the loss of her guesthouse, it was the first summer in years that she didn't have to work around the clock, and she enjoyed it. She and Waldemar didn't last more than a few weeks in boring Rijswijk, and soon enough, they managed to find their way back to Scheveningen, where they belonged. They lived on the upper floor of a sunny villa on the chic Stevinstraat, surrounded by wild dune gardens. The home was owned by one of Rika's good friends who had been widowed a few years earlier and now lived there alone with her five children. In the absence of carpet, Rika stained the wood floor of the new apartment dark brown and traded in the heavy furniture she had brought from the Seafront for lighter, more modern designs. And as she had done at her previous addresses, she made room for her oldest children, who had followed her for so many years like beloved shadows and were now finally starting to take shape in her life.

In August 1942, she wrote to her daughter:

> I told Waldemar, if the lessons work out with little
> Waldy, then we'll buy a piano later, because now that

my kids are grown, I want our home to be a place of
comfort and joy, if only for our dear children. All the
beds are made—because I have five children, and they
all have to be able to come stay with me, with their
husbands, wives, and children, of course! You all are
always welcome here. Really, Johan can sleep here from
now on. And I have made sure there's room for the
children. I told Jan that Ria can most certainly come
for my birthday, and if Aat wants to come, she is more
than welcome. Everyone is welcome now.[60]

Meanwhile, Waldemar was still trying to realize the dream he had
come to Holland to achieve. Once he had earned his degree in English
business correspondence, he began a course in commercial economics
and pursued a license as a chief English correspondent. Then he asked
the Ministry of Education for special permission to be admitted to the
Rotterdam University of Applied Sciences, where his stepson Jan was
studying. The officials, however, were unrelenting: no matter how much
experience or how many degrees Mr. Nods may have had, his junior
high school diploma from the Hendrik School in Suriname was not suf-
ficient for entrance into a university-level program. Shortly afterward,
he found a new job as a bookkeeping correspondent in the nonferrous
metals department of the Ministry of Economic Affairs. His salary was
hardly any higher than it had been before, but the chances for upward
mobility seemed greater.

It was a beautiful but ethereal summer, a calm before the storm.
Scheveningen was strangely quiet without all the beachgoers, and concrete mixers were turning on the beach. The beach was off-limits by
then, but from the balcony of their new apartment, the Nodses could
still smell the sea. If Waldemar and Waldy wanted to go swimming,
they had to take the Blue Tram to the Vliet canal in The Hague. Every
evening, father and son listened to the Radio Oranje broadcasts from

London. Just as they had once traced their vacation routes in the atlas together, they now used the maps to follow military movements. The tides of the war seemed to be turning. In North Africa, the British were driving the German soldiers farther and farther back, and in the Midway Islands in the Pacific, the Americans had dealt the first major blow to the Japanese fleet. In Stalingrad, the Red Army was still valiantly holding out against the "rotten krauts," as Waldy liked to call them. When one of the Van der Lans nieces was visiting and she wondered aloud about when the war would ever be over, Rika laid out her tarot cards in front of her on the table. She studied them seriously for a moment, and then she was certain: it would be over very, very soon.

In November 1942 the announcement came that the rest of Scheveningen would be evacuated so the coast could be fortified. Tens of thousands of people were suddenly forced to move. Rika's friend and her children spent the first days of 1943 traveling to safety in Friesland to wait out the end of the war. Jan considered seeking refuge in the north as well. It had been decided in October that young Dutch men would be deployed for the German war effort, and he had already had a few close run-ins with the *Arbeitseinsatz*—the forced labor—roundups. He left to stay with his brother Wim in Friesland.

In February 1943 the enormous evacuation operation stopped as quickly as it started. Among the approximately twenty-five thousand people still living in the military stronghold was the Nods family. They saw the paradise of Waldy's youth transformed into a haunted landscape right before their eyes. Houses and hotels were boarded shut, the beach was littered with mines and antitank barricades, and the dunes were filled with bunkers. The clocks on Rika's church were sent to Germany to be used in the war effort, and even the red lighthouses were painted in camouflaging colors. Where it had once boasted a sea view, Seafront 56 now looked out over an eight-foot-thick tank wall. In a mysterious fire on March 26, the party hall on the pier was reduced to a grim, charred stockade. All over the seaside town, entire housing blocks were being demolished to make room for an antitank trench with dragon's teeth fortifications. Once completed, the barricade would be more than three miles long and nearly one hundred feet wide, hermetically sealing off the military base from the rest of the world. In the meantime, the once-bustling Scheveningen had fallen so quiet that even the timid nightingales had taken to building their nests there.

It was around this time that Waldy noticed that his mother was housing people in the attic. Even from the first floor, which was half dismantled by then, he'd sometimes hear footsteps or voices coming from upstairs at the oddest hours. This surprised him—surely there weren't any tourists anymore? Only after he was brought home by two German police officers, because he'd gotten in a fight with some boy who had called him a dirty nigger and thrown rocks at him, did his mother decide to tell him the truth. She was scared to death when she saw the officers at her door, she said, because the people living upstairs were Jews, and no one could know that they were there.

***

As the cold weather had set in during the winter of 1942, it became clear that the Nazis were no match for the Russian winter, the tough Red Army, and the stubborn British, so Hitler turned his attention toward his second goal: the fight against international Judaism. Because no matter how many "inferior people"—*Untermenschen*—had been forced to leave Europe, and no matter how many had been annihilated in mass shootings in Eastern Europe, the Jewish race still hadn't fully disappeared. On January 20, 1942, a number of National Socialist leaders had attended a secret conference at an estate on the frozen Wannsee southwest of Berlin to discuss the matter. As conference leader Reinhard Heydrich stressed, it was not enough to hunt them down and starve them out—the strongest would survive and reproduce, planting roots for an even stronger race. The problem needed to be addressed systematically, *gründlich*. And once the Nazi leaders agreed on this fact, they had no trouble developing an efficient strategy to execute their Final Solution.

"Die Pflicht ruft"—duty calls—as the soldier had written in Rika's guest book. With the same sense of duty and devotion, the German people once again followed their führer. On May 3, 1942, the Nazi regime in Holland ordered that no Jew over age six could leave the house without a Star of David clearly visible on their clothing. Just two months later, the Dutch newspapers published a declaration that all *Volljuden* ("full-blooded" Jews) would be sent to work in Eastern Europe. The calls for this massive transport came via the Jewish Council, a consultative body set up by the occupying forces that, in the spirit of democracy, tried to use negotiation to limit the damage of the anti-Jewish policies until the end of the war.

Although the thought of being dragged away from everything they'd ever known and taken to the very place their ancestors had fled from to escape the pogroms was terrifying, the large majority of the 140,000 Dutch Jews still answered the call of the Jewish Council. What else could they do? Hiding was expensive and extremely dangerous, and if you were picked up on the street during a raid, you would be transported directly to Mauthausen, a concentration camp notorious for its terrible treatment of Jews. Moreover, the Jews assumed they wouldn't be the only ones who would have to do their part for the Nazi empire. Unemployed people had already been put to work for the German war effort, and most of the remaining Dutch men had been sent to Germany in large numbers as well. The Jewish Council had been promised that Dutch Jews would receive preferential treatment in the labor camps. And so, the people packed their suitcases with the approved items on the Council's list, cleaned their houses until they sparkled, and locked the doors securely behind them so everything would be intact when they returned.

On July 14, 1942, the first trains left for Westerbork in Drenthe. A camp for escaped German Jews had been set up there before the war, and the Nazis were now using it as a transit camp. Internally, the camp was mostly run by the prisoners themselves; the SS simply supplied the barbed wire and manned the watchtowers around it. From Westerbork, the Nazis operated the exceptionally efficient transportation to Polish labor camps with strange names like Treblinka, Auschwitz, and Sobibor. The deportees weren't told much more than that, but what did you expect? It was wartime and it was far away. And besides, there was hardly anyone left behind in Holland to wait for their letters or news anyway, for the Germans kept the trains running all summer, fall, and winter long, and even into the spring. Everyone had to go: women and children, the elderly and the sick, entire families and neighborhoods, until March 1, 1943, about one year after the Wannsee Conference, when the *Entjudung*, the "Aryanization" of Holland, was virtually complete.

The Stevinstraat, where the Nods family was living, was located on the edge of the Belgisch Park, a neighborhood where many Jews from Antwerp had settled during the First World War. Once the trains to Westerbork started running, the Nodses' world slowly emptied. The streets gradually became deserted, and more and more shops were closed. From the balcony of their house, Waldy would often see sad groups of people being escorted down the street by German soldiers. These were the ones who had tried to hide and been caught. First, they were detained in the Villa Windekind on the Nieuwe Parklaan, the headquarters of the *Judenreferat*, the department responsible for removing all Jews in the Dutch royal capital, and now they were being transported to the prison in Scheveningen, where so many members of the Dutch Resistance were being held that the building had become known as the "Oranje Hotel." Sometimes Waldy spotted familiar faces among the detainees: friends of his father, colleagues of his mother, owners of stores where they used to shop. One fateful day, he was shocked to see their ever-cheerful baker, Rädler, who had often let him and Topsy tag along on his rounds with the baker's cart. Waldy had always considered him a friend. Shuffling down the street in wooden clogs, his black beard long and unkempt, the small man was a pitiful sight to behold.

***

Though the Netherlands had been somewhat passive during the early years of the occupation, resistance was growing now that Dutch men were being sent to Germany, and Dutch Jews were being shipped off to Eastern Europe by the tens of thousands. All over the country, care networks for people in hiding were sprouting up like mushrooms, and underground newspapers and gangs of Resistance fighters were on the rise. At the end of 1942, the regional Resistance networks organized themselves into the Landelijke Organisatie voor Hulp aan Onderduikers, or the LO, a national organization to assist those in hiding. At first, the organization was primarily focused on supporting non-Jewish Dutch people in hiding, but from the spring of 1943 onward, when essentially any person of Jewish descent who had not yet been captured was in critical danger, it increasingly offered help to Jews as well. The demand for safe houses exploded, and the LO often sought houses of people who moved in religious circles. It's therefore likely that Waldemar and Rika got into Resistance work through the Catholic Church.

For Rika and Waldemar were ideal candidates: they had a small family and a large house, they had always counted many Jewish people among their friends, and most of all, they were experienced hosts. Furthermore, they had already been known before the war for their willingness to help and their boundless time and energy for other people. For Waldemar, hospitality was a natural byproduct of his culture; for Rika, it was simply her nature. Together, their urge to welcome people into their home was even stronger. And in general, happy marriages made for better safe houses, because love, unlike suffering, is much more likely to inspire noble deeds.

For Rika, who had spent most of her adult life happily running a guesthouse, taking people into hiding was initially just a continuation of what she had been doing before. It appealed to her need to help people and her sense of justice, and on top of that, it was a good way to earn money. Because, as she wrote in a letter to one of her brothers in 1943, she had lost her prewar wealth along with her guesthouse:

> Money is tight, thank God I don't have any debt. But these days I have to watch every penny. Everything is fine, and we are happy and content. I can't blame myself for the fact that the war has made you rich and me poor. I leave everything in God's hands, and every morning I kneel down and pray for the new day and for new courage and strength. And I will remain cheerful in spite of all the misery.[61]

Host families received ration cards, and in most cases, the LO provided a stipend for each person hiding in their house. This stipend could amount to 45 guldens a month for gentiles and 60 guldens for Jews—no small sum in a time when a decent monthly salary was around 150 guldens.

At first, Waldemar and Rika hardly realized how incredibly dangerous it all was. Pension Walda had always had German guests, and they had always known them to be polite and courteous people. They regarded the Nazis' terror tactics as last-ditch efforts, which would most certainly not be supported by the reasonable people of Germany. At first, the Nodses were amateurs when it came to underground activities. When Henk came to visit his mother on the Stevinstraat, he discovered to his horror that the backside of their secret radio could be clearly seen through the bay window. But Rika dismissed his concerns: surely it wouldn't come to that. A little while later, he found unmade beds and dirty dishes upstairs. Surprised, he asked his mother whose they were, and she replied nonchalantly that they were hiding people in the house. Their guests were out at the moment, she said, getting fish down at the harbor.

***

During the course of 1943, the search for people in hiding intensi-fied and the Resistance professionalized its efforts. Rika and Waldemar came into contact with Kees Chardon, a lawyer from Delft with whom they soon developed a fruitful collaboration. Despite Chardon's young age—he turned twenty-four that year—and small stature, he was one of the most important figures in the South Holland Resistance. At the age of twenty-one, "Crown Kees" had graduated cum laude in law, and his firm in The Hague had been helping Jewish clients ever since, often free of charge. When the people in his care were forced to go under-ground that March, he didn't hesitate to go with them. For, as one of his Resistance friends later put it, "he believed that it was a time when survival came first, and philosophizing came later."[62]

Together with florist and member of the Dutch Reformed Church Ad van Rijs, Kees specialized in what was one of the most difficult tasks in the underground network: finding reliable hiding places for Jews. During the weekly "fair" organized by the provincial department of the LO to match people who needed to go into hiding with families will-ing to take them in, it was easy enough to find places for the "regular laundry"—in other words, the non-Jewish Dutch—especially if it con-cerned a lonely widow or a family with an unmarried daughter who had specifically requested an "eligible bachelor." Not only that, small busi-nesses and farms were usually happy to have a helping hand. But when it came to the "big laundry"—Jewish people—potential host families were considerably less eager. Not only was it more dangerous, but there was also the fact that Jews were generally harder to pass off as members of gentile families. This was partially due to cultural differences and par-tially to the fact that they were often not at their best emotionally, for, unlike the non-Jewish Dutch, they no longer had any savings or a place to call home. Another complication was the fact that some Resistance groups weren't entirely free of anti-Semitism themselves. There was, for example, one group in Rotterdam that refused to help Jewish people in any way, shape, or form, because they believed that the Jews had brought this misery on themselves by crucifying Christ.

Kees Chardon, however, an idealist through and through, traveled far and wide in search of safe houses for "his" Jews and helped hundreds of them find hiding places. Once, when he was urged at an LO meeting to take fewer risks, he replied: "If I'm going to help anyone escape, I'd rather help Jews—preferably in the forbidden zones and after curfew."[63] As an active member of the Resistance, Kees couldn't house Jews for more than a day or two himself because it would be too dangerous for everyone involved, which was how the Nods residence on the Stevinstraat quickly ended up functioning as a transit house where people stayed for both short and longer periods until a more permanent place for them was found in the countryside. Practical support for the Chardon group was provided by Delft police officer Jan van der Sloot, who, together with his Resistance cohorts, raided distribution centers and police stations and hatched plans to free detainees.

As different as Rika and Kees were in terms of age and intellectual background, they spoke each other's language. They were both energetic and emotional by nature, and both courageous to the point of recklessness. "She was a noble woman," wrote one of Rika's secret Jewish houseguests about her hostess. "We spent three months at her place in Scheveningen, and we got along like old friends."[64] Both Rika and Kees found strength in their faith, though she was Catholic and he was Protestant. But no matter how divided the Resistance movement in The Hague was, local churchgoers managed to put their prewar denominational differences aside and work together.

As in peacetime, Waldemar left the daily household business to his wife. Still, Rika didn't make any major decisions without consulting him, and he was well aware of everything going on in their house. He certainly wasn't the only West Indian involved in the Resistance. Members of the Surinamese labor union in Amsterdam were particularly active in helping Jews. Despite that the Nazi doctrine considered people of color grossly inferior, they were generally left alone. There simply weren't enough of them to devise a separate policy—and they even received extra rice rations.

***

Rika ran her illegal guesthouse with as much verve and ingenuity as she had run Pension Walda. Her greatest challenge was collecting enough food without the local shops noticing that she bought a lot for someone with such a small family. She either had to spread out her shopping or only frequent stores run by patriotic shopkeepers. She also tried to procure extra fruits and vegetables on the black market through her brothers. Apparently, they weren't totally unaware of what their sister was up to. In the summer of 1943, she asked them without batting an eye for twenty-two pounds of green beans—"not for canning."[65]

Meanwhile, Rika and Waldemar had caught on to the fact that their activities weren't without danger. While police officers in Amsterdam, for example, were engaged in such frequent sabotage that the Germans eventually stopped trying to use them for their cause, the police force in The Hague remained remarkably law-abiding under the new order. Without protest, officers in The Hague supervised the transport of Jewish prisoners, and some even agreed to work as guards in Westerbork. The Dutch military intelligence service, which had been keeping tabs on suspicious leftist activities before the war, willingly surrendered to the Nazis' clear-cut system after Holland's capitulation. Most agents became members of the NSB, and their department, redubbed the Documentation Service, went to war with members of the Dutch Resistance. This was how Franz Fischer, a virulent anti-Semite and Judenreferat leader, managed to recruit several exceptionally fanatic and professional "Jew hunters" to work for him. His job was facilitated by the fact that the Dutch Resistance network was hanging by a thread: there were so many divisions within the network itself that it was easy for traitors and provocateurs to cause carnage in their ranks. There were even groups, like that of painter Ru Paré, that chose to take their security into their own hands and distance themselves from anything and everything associated with "the organized Resistance."

The most infamous branch of the Documentation Service was the *Jodenploeg*, the Jew-hunting squad, as its members proudly called themselves. The German *Sicherheitsdienst* (SD), the SS intelligence agency, paid them a premium for every Jewish person they delivered to headquarters, and they made a sport of bringing in as many as possible. The group consisted of a dozen men who, like most of the Dutch who sided with the German regime, had felt ignored and frustrated in the Netherlands before the war. In general, they weren't particularly intelligent and thus easily influenced, and thanks to the unusual wartime circumstances, they suddenly found themselves wielding a power they had never had before. Their undisputed leader was the young Maarten Spaans from The Hague. Energetic and assertive, he mercilessly hunted down his prey with the pleasure of a rabbit hunter.

When, on a lovely summer's night, a German truck came to a grumbling halt on the Stevinstraat, right in front of the Nodses' front door, everyone in the house woke with a start. The Jodenploeg had come for them, they were sure of it. Half-dressed, the houseguests ran for their lives, through the big backyard and up to the makeshift hideout they had built in a former sand dune. But when Waldemar opened the front door, he was met not by Dutch police officers or SD agents on the prowl, but by Rika's daughter's fiancé, looking somewhat disheveled after a long journey. It turned out he had run away from the factory in Germany where he had been sent to work and hitchhiked his way back to the Netherlands. Barely had the group recovered from the terrifying incident when a second one occurred, this one more serious than the first. Despite all agreements not to, one of the women hiding in the house decided to venture out onto the street. She was soon recognized in The Hague as a Jew. The residents of the Stevinstraat were immediately warned by telephone, and they quickly dispersed to various locations. It was days before the coast was clear enough to come back.

Shortly afterward—at the end of August 1943—the evacuation of Scheveningen resumed, and the Nods family was forced to move again. After living in a shelter for evacuees in The Hague for a few weeks, they were transferred to an upstairs apartment on the Pijnboomstraat in mid-September. And so, fourteen years after they had photographed each other in the freshly fallen snow on the Azaleastraat, Rika and Waldemar returned to The Hague's "neighborhood of flowers and trees," which was still as bare as ever.

Taking advantage of the fact that, officially speaking, they had five children in their household, Rika managed to secure a two-story apartment, and before long, the underground Pension Walda was up and running again at the new address. The Nods family lived on the lower floor, and the upper floor functioned partially as a transit house and partially as temporary quarters for people who needed a longer-term place to stay, such as the young Jewish couple that was brought to the house in October 1943 by Kees Chardon: Dobbe Franken and her fiancé, Herman de Bruin.

***

A half-century later, Dobbe Franken would recall one period of the war that ended up being the worst of them all—even worse than the terrifying time that came after it—and that was the last months of 1943, when she lived at Pijnboomstraat 63 with her Herman. Though the autumn sunlight still cast a light glow on her red hair and she was still able to walk down the streets of The Hague undisturbed, she had become a gray shadow, a nonperson, someone no longer allowed to exist and who could trust no one.

Once, Dobbe happened to pass by the home of painter Ru Paré, for whom she and her sister had modeled before the war. Her first impulse was to just ring the doorbell to say hello. But she stopped herself short:

what if this woman, like so many others she never would have expected it from, had chosen the other side and was no longer to be trusted? If three years under the Nazis had taught Dobbe anything, it was that even the friendliest of faces could conceal a traitor. So, she walked on, unaware of the fact that Paré and her friends had shepherded dozens of Jews safely through the war, and that had she rung the doorbell, her life—and Herman's—could have been very different.

Dobbe, who was twenty-one years old when the war broke out, was the oldest daughter of the respected Rotterdam judge Maurits Franken and his elegant Russian wife. The Frankens were the picture of a perfectly assimilated Jewish family: enlightened in their ideas, and at the center of a large circle of artistic, intellectual friends. This circle, however, did not dissuade her father from becoming a devoted Zionist. He knew the history of his people all too well and was fully aware of the fact that Jews, no matter how well they managed to assimilate, would always be vulnerable as long as they had no place in the world to call their own. Even still, when the swastika flags were raised all over the Netherlands in 1940, he never thought that he and his family would find themselves in critical danger.

It wasn't long before various anti-Jewish measures were put into effect and Dobbe's father was forced to quit his job, and she had to drop out of school. But, as they used to say to comfort each other, life goes on. Franken made himself useful as a member of the Jewish Council, and Dobbe became a nurse's apprentice at the Portuguese-Jewish hospital in Amsterdam. It was there that she met Herman de Bruin, who was working in the pharmacy after being forced to quit medical school. Thanks to Dobbe's father's work on the Council, both Dobbe and Herman received a much-coveted spot on the "Frederiks List," a list of people who had made significant cultural, intellectual, or social contributions and would therefore be exempt from having to do hard labor in the East. On March 1, 1943, this elite group was detained on the Barneveld estate in the Veluwe, where they were told they could wait out the end of the war. But at the end of September 1943, word was received that the "Barneveld Jews" would be sent to Westerbork that same day. Dobbe's father believed that it was best to calmly comply, but his daughter no longer trusted their so-called protectors. She and Herman tore the Star of David off their clothes, hid until everyone was gone, and made their way to their friends in Amsterdam.

During her summer in the forests of the Veluwe, the atmosphere in the occupied Netherlands had changed dramatically. The Nazis had stopped masquerading as polite civil servants, and the vicious hunt for Jews was on. Raids, executions, and other forms of public terror were the order of the day, and Dobbe and Herman realized that they were putting their friends in Amsterdam in grave danger by staying at their house. Through an acquaintance of Dobbe's father, the runaway couple came into contact with Kees Chardon, who put them up for one night at his home in Delft. The next day, he led them to the upper floor of the Pijnboomstraat in The Hague, where their contact with the outside world was limited to weekly visits from a Resistance worker who delivered ration cards, money, and smuggled letters.

Herman was so noticeably Jewish that Dobbe wouldn't let him out of the house under any circumstances, but she, with her red locks and light skin, could easily pass for Aryan. She did all the shopping and even managed to secure a job as a cleaning lady under the name on her fake identity card, Margreet Spiegelenberg. However, she realized that her new identity wasn't particularly convincing when an eye doctor wrote her a prescription for new glasses and refused payment. "Don't worry about it, ma'am. You have more important things to spend your money on," he said. As friendly a gesture as it was, for Dobbe it was yet another reminder that any human contact was potentially lethal. From then on, she didn't associate with anyone. Not with the constantly changing, albeit clearly Jewish, residents lodged in the other rooms on their floor, and not with the family living below them acting as their landlord. To what extent these people—a white woman, a black man, and their mixed-race son—knew about their situation, she didn't know, nor did she know what their motives were for offering them shelter. And she didn't want to know. Life in the shadows had left her terribly afraid and depressed, and she constantly had to be on her guard.

***

Gerard van Haringen, on the other hand—who arrived at the Pijnboomstraat just a few weeks after Dobbe and Herman—later couldn't recall a single moment when he felt afraid. But he was a special case in more ways than one. Not only was he as blond and Aryan-looking as could be, he had marched in the gray uniform with the dreaded SS symbol on the collar not long before he had arrived. Gerard was only seventeen, practically a child soldier, when he left home for voluntary service in the Waffen-SS. He had envisioned the life of the soldier to be like it was in the propaganda films he had seen at the movies: full of exciting, manly adventures, like jumping from moving army trucks and driving amphibious vehicles on faraway beaches. At that point, he would've done anything to escape the boredom of school and his father's fire-and-brimstone sermons about his poor grades. For as good as Gerard was in physical activities, he had an aversion to anything that required him to use his brain.

During the intense training program at the Nazi base in Munich, he discovered that the reality of serving in the German military was very different from the riveting tales in boys' adventure books. A few of his fellow soldiers-to-be even committed suicide, but the athletic Gerard completed his training with shining colors and was enthusiastically conscripted as a *Panzergrenadier* in the Westland Battalion. It wasn't until he found himself on the Eastern Front, near Kharkiv, Ukraine, that the harsh reality of the war sank in. He contracted dysentery before ever firing a shot and had to be transported back behind the lines by hospital train. The bloody scenes he witnessed in the train, the mutilated and dying soldiers, were enough to convince him to use his first furlough to escape and return to his parents' house in Rotterdam Noord, to the father whose heart he'd broken the day he signed up for the SS.

Van Haringen Senior went to a lot of trouble to find a safe place for his son to hide. If he were found, he would have to go before the military tribunal and would most certainly be shot. Most members of the Resistance didn't want to dirty their hands with an SS deserter, but finally, via an acquaintance, Marcel van der Lans, he came into contact with Kees Chardon, the man who had become a magnet for hopeless cases. This was how Gerard ended up on the Pijnboomstraat. Rika's heart was certainly big enough for such a young soul, who in all his misguided bravado had been easily swayed by the Nazi propaganda. Everyone made rash, stupid mistakes in their youth—she, of all people, knew that.

Gerard found life with the Nods family very much to his liking. Obviously, a former SS agent couldn't be housed with the Jews hiding upstairs, so he was put up in the side room above the stairs and adopted into the family like a son. Aunt Riek was exceptionally caring. She had a solution for everything and was an excellent cook—something a robust, constantly hungry eighteen-year-old like Gerard didn't take lightly. In turn, with his Aryan appearance and strong arms, he was able to help her with the groceries. And he was in absolute awe of his gentlemanly black host. Though Gerard had never been particularly prone to deep thinking, a half-century later, the image of Waldemar remained engraved in his memory. He was, as Gerard later recalled, a man who made you feel calm.

For little Waldy, who was fourteen by now and not so little any-more, Gerard was a sort of replacement for his legendary oldest brother who had never come to see him, and above all, a new friend in a time when almost everything he loved had been taken away from him. Gerard taught him to play chess and guitar, two bright spots in an oth-erwise far-from-happy time. Waldy missed the house on the Seafront, and he missed his buddies whom he had lost touch with since they left Scheveningen, especially since he failed his first year at the Jesuit high school—or as the priests put it, he had been "too playful and did not take it seriously"—and his father moved him to another high school. And most of all, he missed the sea, which was now blocked off by tank trenches, rings of barbed wire, minefields, and other armaments that the Germans had used to transform the once-frivolous seaside town into a stark military base.

Gerard secretly spent Christmas 1943 with his parents at their house in Rotterdam Noord. Meanwhile, in Washington, Commander in Chief Dwight D. Eisenhower was preparing to invade Western Europe; in Italy, the British troops were planning a decisive attack on the Gustav Line in Monte Cassino; and in Russia, the Red Army had finally managed to take back Leningrad. Around that time, one of Rika's sisters came to visit them on Pijnboomstraat with her husband and daughter. They couldn't help but notice the shadowy figures darting out of sight on the stairs, but Rika and Waldemar acted like having these Jewish-looking strangers wandering around their house in these frightening times was the most normal thing in the world. As the visitors walked home in The Hague's dusky afternoon light, Rika's brother-in-law said, "Rika really ought to be more careful."

***

Early in the morning on January 18, 1944, the doorbell rang. It was six thirty, and the street was still cloaked in darkness. Waldemar and Waldy were already awake, but Rika was in bed, suffering from an inflammation of the jaw. Gerard was asleep as well. The downstairs door had been locked for the night, so Waldy went down to open it. He had hardly turned the key, when the door was pushed open with tremendous force. Men in black leather jackets stormed past him and marched upstairs. He felt a pistol pressed into his back. A few seconds later, Gerard awoke to find a large man standing over his bed. His presence filled the entire room. "Are you Jewish?" he asked. When Gerard said no, he was ordered to get dressed. Rika was already up and dressed, and even in the chaos, she still thought to grab a bag of sugar and a pack of margarine from the kitchen. Above their heads, they heard heavy footsteps, doors forced open, and shrieks. Moments later, the upstairs residents came stumbling down the stairs, trembling with fear.

Dobbe, who had been out cleaning that morning, came walking down the street just as it was getting light. She arrived to find a group of onlookers gathered in front of number 63, waiting to watch their neighbors be carted off. Through the crowd, she saw Herman and the men in leather jackets, and she realized that something was wrong, but oddly enough it never occurred to her to flee. The only thing she could think about was the tin of cookies their friends in Amsterdam had sent for Christmas and how it must still be in the wardrobe upstairs. Submissively, she turned herself over to the police, who ushered her into the patrol wagon that was standing by to take them to the police station on the Javastraat. The Nods family was placed together in one cell, but Rika and Waldemar were taken for questioning almost immediately.

For Waldy, the day in the cell was so boring it seemed to last forever. At one point, he wrote a note on the triangular back flap of an old brown envelope that he found in his pocket: "Be brave Ger and see you soon." He folded it up and tossed it into the cell across from him that Gerard van Haringen had disappeared into. It was dark outside the cell window by the time his parents came back. He was shocked at the sight of them; they both looked terribly shaken. At the Villa Windekind, Maarten Spaans was typing up the routine arrest report from the Pijnboomstraat raid:

> In the Nods residence, Nods being the main ten-
> ant of Pijnboomstraat 63, a radio was found that was
> being used by Nods and his family to listen to reports
> broadcast by the enemy. Nods acknowledged this.
> Furthermore, Nods declared that he was aware that he
> had been hiding Jews and a Waffen-SS deserter in his

home. As far as the Jews were concerned, the matter
was mostly handled by his wife. His wife, H. M. J. van
der Lans, refused to make a statement about this.[66]

That morning, Dobbe tried to use her fake name one last time.
But the sergeant on the other side of the table immediately retorted:
"Certainly not. You must be Dobbe Franken." On the table in front of
him was a list of names:

Abraham Cohn, born September 22, 1904, resident of Voorburg
Joseph Polak, born October 18, 1898, resident of Naarden
Herman de Bruin, born June 3, 1918, resident of Amsterdam
Dobbe Franken, born September 1, 1919, resident of Rotterdam[67]

When she saw the list, she knew they had been betrayed.

There was no room for denial for Gerard van Haringen either. The
Nazis knew everything about him: his name, where he lived, his date
of birth, and his status as a deserter. When they asked him what he
had done with his uniform and weapons, he didn't dare to tell them
that he had dumped them in the Bergse lake in Rotterdam. Instead, he
concocted a story that he had swapped his clothes with an acquaintance
at the train station in Utrecht who hadn't passed the German medical
examinations. However, when asked about his fellow residents on the
Pijnboomstraat, he figured that the best strategy was to tell the truth
about what he had seen: that there had always been new people coming
and going in the house.

His interrogator promptly sent word to the Jodenploeg members
who had stayed behind to search the house and instructed them to keep
watch for another night or two—you never know who might come
by. When asked how he ended up at the Pijnboomstraat in the first
place, Gerard simply answered the question—after all, he barely knew
Chardon, what harm could it do?

***

That evening, a little after ten o'clock, the doorbell rang at Chardon's law office on the Spoorsingel in Delft. His family lived in the adjoining house. Kees was sitting in the living room with a few people to whom he had just issued fake documents. When he opened the front door, the Jodenploeg stormed in and took over, yet he still managed to sound the alarm across the quiet canal. His shouts were heard by someone hiding a few houses away who then proceeded to warn several people by telephone.

Kees's parents and two of his sisters were reading in the salon above the office and didn't hear a thing. Only when the door was flung open and the men in leather jackets suddenly stormed into the room did they know they were under siege. The other invaders barreled up the stairs to the attic, where they found a little girl in one of the bedrooms. Although she had been instructed to state her last name as Chardon, she was so shocked that she muttered her own: Betty Springer, twelve years old. "A highly gifted child, she wrote her own poems," one of Kees's sisters later recalled. The agents congratulated each other: another Jew, another payout.

Downstairs, Maarten Spaans made a few valuable discoveries of his own. In Kees's desk, which had been left open, he found address lists, several blank and falsified identity papers, as well as ration coupons from the City of The Hague and the employment office. "The Delft lawyer Cornelis Chardon enabled the escape of Jews on a large scale," as the SD report would later describe Chardon's broad efforts to help Jews hide and escape.[68] Kees made one last attempt to escape that evening through the sunroom door, but with his small frame he was no match for Spaans and his sidekick. As punishment, he was kicked and beaten. A little while later, backup arrived from Villa Windekind in the form of a few German and Dutch SD agents. Kees's interrogation lasted the rest of the night, during which his arm was broken, among other things, and around four o'clock in the morning he made one last hopeless attempt to flee but was caught and beaten unconscious. Shortly afterward, the residents of the Spoorsingel were taken to Villa Windekind.

Waldemar, Rika, and Waldy had spent the night together in their cell. The next morning—Wednesday, January 19—they were picked up. They were seated on a wooden bench in the hall and guarded by German soldiers. They were not allowed to speak to each other, but Rika still nudged her son, who was sitting between the two of them, and whispered: "Here, give this to Papa, because we probably won't be seeing each other for a while." She pressed Waldemar's wedding ring into his hand; in the chaos of the previous morning, she had managed to snatch it from the bathroom table. Waldy managed to pass the ring to his father, even though it got him a snarl and a threatening gesture from the guard. A little while later, one of the agents beckoned Waldy from the bench and led him toward the exit. He was shoved outside, back into the free world.

Waldy's uncle Bob, his mother's youngest brother, was waiting for him, looking as white as a sheet. When Rika hadn't shown up for a family birthday party the day before, he had called the house. When the phone was answered by a complete stranger, they immediately knew that something was terribly wrong. Two of Rika's sisters went to the Pijnboomstraat the next day and found that the house had been sealed. They heard from the neighbors that the Nodses had been detained. Bob called and received permission to come pick up his nephew. He took Waldy to his grandparents' house. In the meantime, Bertha, who had been transferred to Nijmegen six months earlier, found out what happened. She sent word to her brother Henk and their father in Groningen. The next day, Henk buried the thick stack of letters and cards he had received from his mother over the years under a tile in the bike shed behind the garden. You never know—perhaps the Nazis would come looking for evidence.

On Friday, January 21, an official report was issued stating that Rika and Waldemar had been incarcerated in the *deutsche Polizeigefängnis*, also known as the Oranje Hotel. It was decided that Waldy, who was still staying with his grandparents, would return to school the following Monday. That weekend, he went back to the Pijnboomstraat to collect his schoolbooks and some clothes. The front door of the house had been sealed off, which made Waldy's house key useless, but he was still able to climb in via a side window. Once inside, he wandered through his parents' house. Never had it been so still. His footsteps echoed through the empty rooms. Most of their household items had already been packed up and placed at the top of the stairs, ready to be picked up. Only then did it occur to him that his parents probably wouldn't be coming home for a long time.

The next week, Waldy showed up at the gate of the Oranje Hotel with a basket full of treats in the hopes that he would be able to give them to his parents himself. But the guard refused. He could leave the basket, but he could not see his parents. The two people who made up Waldy's entire world—his mother with her soft arms and his calm, strong father—were swallowed up in that giant stone building.

***

On Thursday, January 27, 1944, nine days after the raid on the Pijnboomstraat, a train bound for Westerbork left from the Scheveningen prison. Inside was a week's worth of bounty collected by The Hague's notorious Jew hunters—about seventy-five people in total, of whom fifteen had been rounded up thanks to the Chardon raid. Among them was fifty-three-year-old Leopold Nabarro, a Jewish man who, along with his Dutch protector, had been captured the night after the Nods raid.

At Westerbork, Dobbe and Herman were awaited by her parents and sister. They had heard the bad news via the underground information network and hoped that the couple would still be counted among the hard-labor-exempt Barneveld Jews. However, like everyone captured in the raids, Dobbe and Herman were taken to the barracks marked *S* for *Strafe*, or punishment. From there, they would be among the first to be sent to the East. Not even two weeks later, on Tuesday, February

8, their trains arrived. Among the many hundreds of people who were loaded into the freight cars were Dobbe, Herman, and the other Jews picked up at the Pijnboomstraat, as well as Betty Springer, who had been reunited with her little brother at Westerbork.

The trains were overcrowded and unheated, and the only sanitary facilities were two big barrels per car: one for drinking water and the other for human waste. On February 11, the train arrived at the station of the Polish town of Auschwitz. Outside, everything was frozen, and there was a peculiar odor in the air that no one could quite put their finger on. When Dobbe clambered out of the car, a fellow passenger asked her to grab a small child who was still on the train. With the toddler in her arms, Dobbe walked toward the camp, until they reached the checkpoint, where an SS officer was assessing the newcomers. He took one look at Dobbe and pointed to the right, to the side for the elderly, sick, and mothers and children, including Betty Springer, the little girl who wrote such good verse. Instinctively, Dobbe set the child down and explained to the officer in her best school German that she was not the little one's mother. *Gut,* muttered the SS agent and motioned for the child to go right and her to go left.

Only then, at that place and in that moment, did Dobbe begin to realize that she and Herman had been running from something far worse than being robbed of their freedom or being forced to do heavy labor, that her father and his colleagues at the Jewish Council had been much more naive than she ever could have imagined, and that, with that impulsive choice she had just made, she had saved her own life. For the first time, she realized that something inconceivable was going on, something entirely unprecedented: the systematic annihilation of human beings. Hitler was dead serious about his plans for the German people to take over the entire world, and it turned out he was equally serious about his deranged plan to rid the world of Jews. This was not where life went on, this was where it stopped.

7

Rika's Eyes

Waldemar and Rika celebrated their seventh wedding anniversary in Scheveningen, albeit in the deutsche Polizeigefängnis, where Waldemar was being held in cell 403 and Rika in cell 382. Paula Chardon, Kees's sister, was imprisoned in that same cell on January 20, 1944. After undergoing interrogation at Villa Windekind, Paula, with her other arrested family members, was brought to the Oranje Hotel, "walking by empty houses through empty streets," as she wrote in her diary.[69]

> Hardly had the door been opened, and you were shoved in without a word and the door was closed behind you. Inside, I saw an old lady, two young Jewish women and a woman with fiery eyes. I was exhausted and sat right down. They asked where I was from. "From Delft," I said. Suddenly, the woman with the black eyes jumped up and exclaimed, "Are you a Chardon?" "Yes," I replied. She hugged me and cried, "I'm Mrs. Nods!" How happy I was.[70]

Rika and Paula's Jewish cellmates were two good friends from Limburg. "They were always happy and in good spirits. They took care of everything," Paula wrote.[71] Thanks to them, the new residents of cell 382 managed to adjust to daily life in a space designed for one: six and a half feet by about ten feet in surface area and thirteen feet in height. The lights came on at six thirty in the morning. They would wash up as best they could in a makeshift sink, clean their cell, and have breakfast. Then it was a matter of making it through the long day. One of the Jewish women cut thirty-two pieces from a bit of cardboard and drew figures on them with a hairpin, so Rika could read her cellmates' fortunes.

Another daily activity was reciting names and addresses. "Each newcomer received one or two addresses from each cellmate. Whoever got out first would send their news and greetings," Paula wrote.[72] Beyond that, they read whatever they could find and scratched words into the already message-covered wall with a spoon:

> No rabble
> In this can
> Only Dutch glory
> I'll be damned.

And:

> However trying the day,
> Or hard the separation,
> We're one day
> Closer to liberation.

To the wall, Rika added: "Improving the world starts with improving yourself," a motto inspired by the radio priest Henri de Greeve, which she liked so much she had it on a tile on the wall at home.

Around eight o'clock in the evening, the cellmates got ready for bed. Their beds consisted of thickly packed straw mattresses on the floor and a folded coat as a pillow. Then the lights went out and what Paula referred to as "the cozy part" began.

> Until ten o'clock the prisoners would sing their hearts out, pass around letters, exchange news. Every cell had something to talk about. It was like a boarding school. Around 9:30 it would start to quiet down and at 10 the tapping would start. It went like this: on the other side of the wall, someone would tap the Morse code. Aunt Bep, our Morse code expert, would go to the wall and tap back. The first question was whether new people had arrived. That was the case in our cell and in cell 383: Wanda, Mrs. Nods and me. Then they would ask where we were from and if there was any news.[73]

The only breaks from the daily monotony of prison life were showers and moments of fresh air—each once a week—and the distribution of packages from the International Red Cross, which contained food products that hadn't been seen in the occupied Netherlands for years, like real chocolate. But there were terrifying moments as well, like when the air raid siren sounded on January 23 as thousands of Allied planes thundered overhead, and the entire prison prayed that the base in Scheveningen wouldn't be the target that night.

The next morning, Rika was taken by a guard who was known among the prisoners as *"das germanische Edelweib,"* the "Germanic noblewoman."

> Around 11:30 (interrogation time), the door opened. The Edelweib shouted, "Nods!" And off went Aunt Riek. Oh, how her eyes were filled with dread. We kept

her rations in the "hay chest" (two mattresses we used
to keep food warm) and turned to our reading. She
came back around three o'clock: completely pale with
an ice-cold expression on her face. She was in total
panic. What an interrogation it had been! She needed
to clean up before she could talk about it. She was
so shaken that she'd had an accident. It turned into a
happy washing party.

Then Aunt Riek started to tell us what happened: it
was horrible, and, in the end, she got hit by Kappie from
Windekind *with a long curtain rod*! We looked and saw a
big mark by her right ear—that sadist almost bashed her
head in. He hit her arm too. Imagine hitting a woman,
a mother of five children! Aunt Riek was upset the entire
evening and for days after. She laid down and prayed for
hours (she was a good Roman Catholic) that she would
never be taken into interrogation again.[74]

To a certain extent, those who had been so certain that the occupiers would never resort to the most primitive forms of terror had been
right. For just as the disciplined German soldiers preferred not to dirty
their hands with hunting Jews themselves, they left the interrogations
about *"Judensachen"*—or Jewish matters—to the Dutch in their service.
One of the most famous among them was twenty-eight-year-old Kees
J. Kaptein, also known as "Kappie." As a child in the Dutch East Indies,
Kaptein had been systematically humiliated and abused by his father,
and now the former fighter on the Eastern Front took great pleasure
in the fear of those in his custody and enjoyed the power he had over
them. Later, he would brag about the fact that he got 99 percent of his
victims to talk within a month. He described his method as follows:
"First I'd simply ask—then I'd threaten—then deep knee bends—then
a few punches, taps as I like to call them."[75]

Sometimes Kaptein would go so far in exercising his power that even his German superiors would tell him to take it easy. But he was proud of his reputation and of the fact that Radio Oranje had specifically warned people about him in one of their reports. He liked to introduce himself to his new victims with: "I am Kees Kaptein, the greatest Jew crusher in the Netherlands!" Women had it particularly rough with him. From the younger ones, he would try to solicit sexual favors while preaching about his role as a "patron of humanity." And the older ones he would humiliate, especially if they were guilty of what he considered "racial disgrace," in other words, consorting with Jewish men. He would shout and hit, force them to do hundreds of deep knee bends or to walk around a pillar until they literally fell to the floor. For the ones who talked, Kees harbored a kind of satisfied contempt, and it wasn't unusual for him to let those who had done favors for him go free or to relieve them of a few months' punishment. But the few who refused to recognize his omnipotence by pleading and praying for mercy would make him so furious that he would vent his rage on them with his bare fists, the butt of his gun, or an iron curtain rod.[76]

Rika belonged to the last category of victims. She wasn't trying to be heroic, it was simply her nature. Never had she given in to pressure, threats, or fits of anger—not from her parents, not from Willem Hagenaar, and not from the world. And she certainly wasn't about to give in to a man like Kaptein, who was young enough to be her own son. Just as she had done on the day she rode by her parents' house in her wedding dress, and just as she had done as she waved to her husband after picking up her children at The Hague station, Rika looked her interrogator straight in his pale blue eyes. And the more he tried to intimidate her and insult her about her relationship with a black man, the more adamantly she refused to answer his questions. The only thing she wanted to tell him was that she, and she alone, was responsible for hiding people in the house on the Pijnboomstraat—her husband didn't even know about it. And Kees Kaptein was racist enough to believe her—surely such a "dumb nigger" could have been nothing more than this woman's plaything.

The interrogation that Waldemar endured that same morning was child's play compared to what Rika had faced. When he saw her that afternoon in the waiting room at Windekind, he was deeply shocked. "I would have never thought they would treat you like that, Rika," as he later wrote.[77] That evening Paula noted in her diary:

> But for Rika, what made up for everything was that she had seen her husband! They were escorted from Windekind to the jail together. He was a dreadful sight. He was West-Indian looking and now, with such a long beard and no collar, he looked like a bushman.[78]

After all that Rika and Waldemar had been through, they never would have thought that they would have the chance to walk through Scheveningen side by side like they did that day. Together, they traversed the map of their shared history, the sea murmuring in the background and the seagulls screeching overhead. But this time, they were both handcuffed and surrounded by armed soldiers. Over Scheveningen's iconic Kurhaus Hotel was a red swastika flag flapping triumphantly in the wind.

***

A few days after Rika's first interrogation, a cargo train full of Jewish people left for Westerbork.

> At 11:30 all the cells were opened, and the Jews had to get ready. It was horrible. Before they left, Aunt Riek and I split all the food we had. It was the one last thing we could do for them. And then the two of us stayed behind, both in awe of what had just happened. The

prison seemed deserted. It was completely silent, even the babies and children were gone. That afternoon, we got a special treat (because the jail was Jew-free, of course)—white beans and string beans. We couldn't finish a single pan between the two of us. That night Aunt Riek had [a] strange dream: a bunch of cats were lying on top of her. They were crawling all over the bed. I was awakened by a scream of terror.[79]

On February 1, 1944, Paula was released unexpectedly. She was free to go home to Delft, where her mother and sister—both recently discharged as well—were waiting for her. Her father, her brother Kees, and the Nods couple were kept behind to await their trials. In theory, this fact alone was no reason to panic, because officially the punishments for helping Jews were fairly mild—twelve months for men, six for women—and most of them were served at Camp Vught, which was known for being relatively humane.

Police Chief Rauter had had this camp built near Den Bosch in 1943 as a gesture to the Dutch people, so that Dutch political prisoners wouldn't have to be sent to the infamous German concentration camps. It was a sort of model camp: the regime was strict but fair, the food was good, and abusing prisoners was forbidden. When more than eighty women were forced to spend the entire night crammed into two small cells as a punishment—which resulted in ten deaths from suffocation—those responsible were dragged before the disciplinary court. Political prisoners often held positions of power within the camp hierarchy themselves, as the best jobs in the camp were reserved for good patriots, which, especially for Resistance fighters, made the Dutch concentration camp highly preferable to the monotonous boredom, nagging uncertainty, and constant threat of further questioning they faced in prison. "I would very much like to be sent to Vught to work as early as this month," as Kees Chardon wrote to his family.[80]

On February 23, Kees, his father, and Waldemar were indeed sent to the camp in Brabant by train. "Kees was cheerful. He found Vught really quite pleasant," recalled a fellow inmate later. The young lawyer was more worried about the people he had helped hide. "Keep watch over my sheep," he wrote to a cousin who had taken over his work.[81] Little did he know that a large portion of his flock had already been sent to the gas chambers in Auschwitz.

Barely one hundred years after Waldemar's grandmother had managed to free herself from the bondage of slavery, her own grandson was taken as a slave. Upon arrival at Vught, he was numbered, underwent a medical examination, and then was shaved bald and dressed in a blue-and-gray-striped jumpsuit, matching cap, and wooden shoes. He received a food bowl tied to a cord that he had to wear around his waist, and he slept on a plank in a large barrack designed to house two hundred and fifty men.

Shortly after his arrival, Waldemar was assigned to an *Aussenkommando*, or subcamp, that had to dig an antitank trench on the Wouwse plantation near the Belgian-Dutch border. The forced laborers were lodged in a former agricultural college in Roosendaal and guarded by German prisoner functionaries, also known as "Kapos." "We can skip this one," they would say to Waldemar as they handed out the soap. He let their words slide off his back, just as he did when his fellow prisoners teased him good-naturedly. When it started getting dark, the guys would bump into him and say, "You've got to smile, otherwise we can't see you!" Most of them had never seen a black man, and among themselves they had concluded that their intriguing fellow prisoner must have owned a nightclub at a fashionable seaside resort.

Hard outdoor labor was a drastic change for someone who was used to working in an office, but Waldemar was tough and in good shape. His greatest concern was for Rika. He fervently hoped that the Germans would be satisfied with punishing him alone as the primary tenant of the house on the Pijnboomstraat, and that they would let his wife return home safely to their son.

Vught, March 5

Dear Riek or Jo,

If you receive this letter, I hope you are finally back at home. Vught is a relief after the tiny cell in Scheveningen. It has been a major transition, from spending the whole day inside and now the whole day outside in the fresh air. The barracks are tidy with running water and toilets and good beds. You meet many people here. All different types, and we are occupied all day long.

Today we received a Vught package, which makes a big difference in terms of food, because you're always hungry from working outside. They treat us fine here as long as you stick to the rules. I'm urgently in need of the following: towel, washcloth, toothbrush, old socks, pullover, old rags for handkerchiefs, cream or Vaseline, soap, and please send tobacco or cigarettes if you can spare them and things for sandwiches, but that's not absolutely necessary, and also my old wool scarf.

Were you able to work things out?

And Waldy, how are you doing? Have you been keeping an eye on my tobacco for me? Are things going well at school?

Jo, maybe you could send me a few things if Rika isn't back yet, the uncertainty is the worst part for me.

Yours sincerely, Waldemar[82]

But Kees Kaptein was far from through with the stubborn woman from The Hague who provoked him with her eyes. After one of the people who had been hiding on the Pijnboomstraat declared that "Mrs. Nods-van der Lans is connected to Mr. Chardon, who worked together with her to hide many Jews in The Hague and elsewhere," he was sure he'd picked up the trail of a major underground network. And when an Amsterdam Resistance fighter confessed under torture to be under "Chardon in The Hague, head of the illegal movement there," Kees was brought back to Scheveningen. He was promised that he would be returned to Vught within a week, but it ended up being six months, which he mostly spent in solitary confinement in the so-called death cells, where his only contact with his fellow prisoners was via heating pipes and holes in the wall.

Kaptein did everything he could to extract information from his prisoner. He used an agent provocateur to smuggle Kees's letters to his family from prison—only after they had been carefully scrutinized at Windekind for any incriminating information. When Kees discovered that he had been a victim of deception, he was devastated and would spend many more months brooding over the fact that his misplaced trust probably cost people their lives. It was well known in the prison that Kees was tortured on a regular basis. To his family he wrote:

> I'll be silent to the grave. Was interrogated 3x again.
> My condition isn't good, but I'm staying strong and
> trusting God. I still long deep in my heart for fresh
> air and work at Vught. And I still hold on to the hope
> that my other "sheep" have been spared. And that the
> work is progressing.[83]

Kees's Resistance friends proposed to his parents that they try to set him free, but his father considered it too risky. He thought it better to just wait—the end of the war couldn't be that far off.

On May 1, the primary leaders of the Chardon group were sentenced. Both Kees and Rika would serve life for conspiracy and large-scale *Judenhilfe*, aiding Jewish people. Waldemar, who had received a milder sentence of confinement for the duration of the war, tried to lift his wife's spirits in a letter:

Vught, March 7

Dear Jo,

Got your last letter with the letter from Riek. Yes, it's pretty tough to be in such a small space for so long. Will you send her my greetings and tell her that she has to *stay strong* and that once we're free again, we'll most certainly visit Brabant—that's a great idea. Nice that you were able to see her, Bob. Try again from time to time, seeing people from the outside brings courage. How are mother and father doing? Good, I hope, and are you doing better, Jo? And Bertie, have you really got as much tobacco as you said in your letter? You could catch thousands of men in here with all that stuff.

Dinie and Jan, thanks for your package, everything was delicious. The pineapples, in particular, were a big surprise. Sis, the rye bread was wonderful, how are things at the fire department? Greetings to Johan and Jan & Henk, I have to write in telegram style, running out of space. Got another package with homemade bread, cake, cheese, etc. sent by Mien, I think, the paper was torn. Thank you very much, you all are truly spoiling me.

And now, Waldy, it's great to hear you are doing so well, son, but a D- in history and a D+ in Dutch is bad. Study harder, do your book reports and make sure that you pass, otherwise I'll come home and twist your ears.[84]

On May 10, exactly four years since the start of the war, Rika was taken to Vught to serve out her sentence. Thanks to the patriotic guards at the prison in Scheveningen, her family was informed of her transfer, and Bob was able to catch a glimpse of his oldest sister on the platform of the Staatsspoor station. Rika tossed a hastily scribbled letter to him:

Thursday, May 10, 1944

> In the train
> > Hello dear children
> > Hello Father and Mother
> > Hello dear brothers and sisters
> > A big kiss to all of you
> > I'm going to Vught
> > to my sweet husband
> > pray for us often
> > stay strong
> > You know I'll be tough
> > Your loving mother
> > Rika[85]

Waldemar was indeed back in the main camp because the Roosendaal subcamp had been discontinued once again. At Vught, contact between the male and female divisions was strictly forbidden, but there were numerous ways to work around this. There was plenty of smuggling of letters and goods, and there were spots along the barbed wire fence where men and women could call to each other. When the female prisoners marched to their work posts in the morning, they could wave to the men still standing at roll call.

It's certain that Rika and Waldemar saw each other at least once this way. In the sea of bald heads in prison uniforms, Rika was able to easily spot her husband's dark face. But though they were now at a safe distance from Kees Kaptein's fists and curtain rod, they were not outside his sphere of influence. And, as confirmed in a statement by one of his later victims, he had certainly not forgotten about them. As another prisoner later recalled: "He boasted about the fact that he had taken down Chardon's rotten bunch of troublemakers, and he said that he had sent Kees and the others to Germany."

Ten days after her arrival at Vught, Rika scanned the roll call in vain for a glimpse of that dark face. On May 19 at 5:45 in the evening, Waldemar, or the "black case," as Kaptein had branded him, was subject to a medical examination and then loaded into a cargo train along with nine others. The train was headed in the same direction he had traveled seventeen years earlier on the SS *Oranje Nassau*—north-northeast.

***

Five days later, on Wednesday, May 24, the small load from Vught arrived at a large concentration camp southeast of the northern German port city of Hamburg. The Neuengamme concentration camp had been set up six years earlier at an abandoned brickyard to be used as a subcamp of the Sachsenhausen concentration camp. But after Hitler ordered in 1942 that all prisoners contribute to the war effort by serving hard labor for twelve hours a day, the *Reichsführer* Heinrich Himmler, who as police chief was responsible for prisoner policies, gave the camp an independent status. As terror increased in the occupied zones, the number of prisoners rose, and Neuengamme expanded rapidly. It eventually established various subcamps of its own at nearby businesses. The main camp was reasonably well equipped, with a chapel, a hospital, and even a small library, but although it was designed to hold five thousand prisoners, by the spring of 1944, it was home to ten thousand. As Allied forces steadily advanced through Europe, the stream of newcomers swelled: the day Waldemar arrived, another shipment came in carrying at least 1,880 French prisoners from Compiègne.

It was immediately clear to Waldemar that in the huge, overpopulated Neuengamme camp, different rules applied, and the place made Vught seem almost friendly. The camp hierarchy was dominated by German criminals, who wore a green triangle. They had been there the longest and had secured the best jobs for themselves as Kapos. Armed with clubs, they maintained order in the filthy, overcrowded barracks according to the rules of the underworld and the survival of the fittest. The newcomers were shaved from head to toe, deloused, and outfitted with a striped prison uniform. Waldemar's was marked with a red triangle, signifying that he was a political prisoner. The metal plate he was forced to hang around his neck bore the number 32180, meaning that more than 32,000 people had been there before him.

Like the slave plantations, the German concentration camps went down in history as black holes that sucked people in with no regard for them as human beings. Still, these places also had an order all their own. Individual characteristics such as age, physical condition, and social skills played a significant role in a person's lot. The Dutch often had a relatively difficult time in the German camps because, unlike the Russians and Poles, for example, they hadn't been tempered by hard work and too little food from a young age, and they weren't at all used to having to fight for themselves.

Waldemar did, however, have a few things working in his favor, such as the fact that he had arrived at Neuengamme in the spring of 1944. Indeed, the camp was already overcrowded, and most of the newcomers were sent directly to the anonymous mass units in the notorious subcamps, but the main camp was still organized enough that a person could get noticed and secure a good position. And Waldemar stood out. In an environment designed to strip people of their identity and reduce them to an amorphous mass, Waldemar's skin color ensured that he was never just a number. He remained an individual, a person, and that fact alone provided him with extra opportunities. Even though the Nazi propaganda spewed nothing but contempt for the black race, for most

Germans—their country having had hardly any colonies and thus no citizens of color—a black man was extremely exotic.

Three Africans from the French colonies who also arrived at Neuengamme in the spring of 1944 feared for the worst, but as many survivors note, the SS men were just curious to see these beings they considered animals up close. They were, in fact, not scary beasts, they were something unusual, quite different from the other *Untermenschen*. They were hardly human at all. One camp survivor recalled how the SS men had rubbed the dark Senegalese man's skin to see if the color would change. A little while later, an SS officer saw them in the shower and remarked what beautiful athletes they were. They probably reminded him of the Olympic Games in Berlin. Another time, an SS man stood in a factory for a half hour watching in utter surprise as one of the so-called "chimpanzees" turned out to be capable of reading and understanding complicated German plans and carrying them out precisely.

One of the black Frenchmen had been famous as a boxer in Paris and was exalted as a camp mascot. On Sunday afternoons, the camp director organized boxing matches in which he would challenge people to take the Frenchman on. In order to keep their mascot's powerful physique in top condition, they exempted him from hard labor and assigned him one of the highly desirable jobs in the kitchen. And even though the elegant Waldemar was a completely different sort of black man, he, too, must have attracted attention upon arrival with his perfect German and proper ways. He carried himself like a dancer and, even in his striped prison jumpsuit, managed to look dignified.

On July 2, 1944, approximately six weeks after he arrived at Neuengamme, Waldemar sent his first letter home—in German, due to censoring.

> Dear Jo, surely you never imagined that you would
> receive a letter from me in German. A big surprise for

me as well. How is everyone doing, how are your parents, and Riek and my son Waldy? How are you?

I'm well, although I would have preferred to stay
in Holland, as you can understand. It is very different
here than it was at home, and I have had to start all
over again. Would you please send my shaving kit with
razors, soap and shaving brush, as well as some socks?
Have you heard anything from Riek? I wrote a few letters to her in Holland, and I definitely saw her once.

Write back soon, and Waldy, you too. Many warm
regards to everyone, Waldemar[86]

The French boxer apparently felt so confident of his position as the
Sunday afternoon entertainment that he, egged on by a fellow prisoner,
was stupid enough to poke fun at a German Kapo. The next day he was
transferred to one of the worst subcamps; a few months later he was
dead. But Waldemar knew how to adapt—that he had learned in his
first years in Holland. He wasn't one to provoke, and, no matter the
circumstances, he stuck to his good manners and proper demeanor.
His red triangle and trilingual abilities came in handy as well, because
there was an active shadow leadership among the political prisoners,
just as there had been at Vught. These prisoner functionaries occupied
a number of key positions within the camp's administration, and thanks
to the growing lack of SS personnel around this time, they managed
to expand their influence and keep many of their comrades out of the
rougher subcamps.

Thanks to the influence of his fellow prisoners, Waldemar was put
to work in the camp's post office in mid-July, where he translated and
wrote letters for fellow prisoners. As part of the camp's administration,
he was now a member of the camp elite. He was moved from a barrack
where he had to share a bed with three men and sleep with one eye
open to guard his possessions to Barrack 1, which was designated for

prisoners who associated with SS guards on a daily basis. This barrack was relatively clean and safe, and he even got his own bed. His second letter, which was sent three weeks later, was noticeably more cheerful:

Neuengamme, July 23, 1944

Dear Jo,

Today is Sunday, letter-writing day, which is always nice. I am eagerly awaiting your letter and for news about Riek and the rest of you all. Is everything good with you and the family?

Things are going better here, you can write to Riek and tell her that she shouldn't worry, that I'm fine, although I'm in need of everything, but that will come too.

Now Waldy, my son, how are you doing? Whether or not you passed, you're now on vacation. Play lots of sports and study hard. Write back soon and send me a cigarette lighter, one of those little 25 cl. ones. And Jo, please don't forget to send my shaving kit[,] a tooth-brush and tobacco.

Greetings to the whole family and friends and especially to your parents and yourself.

Take good care,
Waldemar[87]

Rika endured several terrible weeks after Waldemar suddenly disappeared from Camp Vught. "Where is my husband?" she asked in every letter and note she managed to send home. "Where is my husband?" she kept asking during a visit with her brother Marcel that, after a great deal of hemming and hawing, he was finally permitted to make. Only after Waldemar's first letter from Neuengamme arrived did she calm down a little bit: at least she knew her husband was still alive. Now she could focus on her own circumstances, which had also improved since she left the prison in Scheveningen. She enjoyed the sun and the fresh air, the camaraderie with all the other women around her, the relative freedom, and above all, being far away from the threat of Kaptein's interrogations.

The political prisoners had managed to get Rika assigned to a work post at Philips, an electronics company that had been hiring camp labor since 1943. Her official job was to assist with mechanical flashlight and condenser manufacturing and radio repair, but in reality, that was a cover for her real work, which was to help see as many Dutch compatriots through the war as possible. The workers were handpicked by the prisoners themselves, who considered "usefulness"—or in other words, one's support for the cause—as a primary criterion.

The production numbers were of little concern to Philips, and the forced laborers could spend part of their eleven-hour shift sleeping in peace. Although the operation was kept on a much shorter leash after the Dutch supervisor was fired in June for "sabotage" and replaced by a German engineer, the system remained alive and well.

Meanwhile, Rika's family, especially her daughter, made sure that Rika, who had always been such a lover of good food, remained well stocked in prison. With the combination of Red Cross packages and the daily hot meal served at Philips, the prisoners often ate better than the people outside the camp. Sometimes they even flushed the camp meals down the toilet because they couldn't finish them. And in terms of contact with the home front, Rika didn't have anything to complain about either. There were plenty of letters exchanged between Vught and the outside world. In addition to the censored letters that the prisoners were allowed to send home twice a month, countless notes were smuggled out through the camp laundry and via released prisoners. Rika even managed to send her children handmade birthday presents, such as an embroidered cross and a plexiglass charm in the shape of a tear, fashioned from materials found in the camp's airplane demolition unit.

Vught, July 17, 1944

Dear Father, Mother, brother and sisters, my dear sweet children. Received Waldy's postcard this morning and Jo's letter last Wednesday, very happy to get them and even happier that Waldy has passed to the next grade. Wonderful Waldy, Papa will be so happy to hear it. It's now Sunday, and I haven't received *any* packages this week, the last one from Marcel arrived 8 days ago. I was really happy with it, and thank you all so much, I hope this week's package hasn't been lost, that would be terrible. Make sure it's not heavier than 3 kilograms, otherwise it'll be sent back. If you want to send fruit or tomatoes and cucumbers, you can send a separate fruit parcel every week. If you do, you have to mark it as "fruit parcel."

I hope you all are in the pink of health, I'm doing just fine. Only I long for you all. I hope that you'll write back soon and that you've received good news from Waldemar, because I really long for him too. I hope that I can see you all soon, I've been away from home for six months this week. Pray that we will see each other again soon, I'm out of space, sending a big kiss to all of you, and love to all our friends and acquaintances from your loving mother and to all of you, Riek *see you soon* bye!![88]

There was no shortage of illegal radios in the Philips factory, and the Vught prisoners were able to closely monitor the war's progress. After invading northern France on June 6, 1944, the Allies launched the invasion of Western Europe. Slowly but surely, the American, British, and Canadian armies fought their way across the Continent that summer.

Again and again, it was the Allies' supremacy in the skies that determined their victory, with special thanks to Waldemar's homeland of
Suriname, which provided 60 percent of the bauxite needed for the
Allied air fleet. The prison in Scheveningen was evacuated the day after
the invasion. Those detained for milder offenses were sent home, and
the more serious cases, like Kees Chardon, were placed in the isolated
and heavily guarded bunker complex at Vught.

By mid-August, the Americans had reached Paris. The Third Reich
had yielded to their demands, and the camp's rumor mill was turning
at full speed. The air was sparkling with optimism—surely, liberation
must be right around the corner.

Vught, August 20, 1944

Dear Father, Mother, brothers and sisters, my dear
sweet children. First of all, happy birthday to Jan.
And I hope that this is the last family birthday I am
unable to attend. The next birthday on this list is my
Waldemar's. Oh, it will be such a party if we can all
celebrate it together. My dear little Waldy, keep waking
up early and celebrate Holy Mass for your dear mother
every day, pray for Peace to come soon for *all* people! I
hope that Waldemar has received his mail and package
by now. Did H. get a reply from him yet?

No postcard from Waldy this week. How can that
be? Sis, your excellent fruit parcel was wonderful. It
was almost like you were visiting me in person. Aunt
Bert, thanks a lot for all your sweet care, everything
arrived just fine, I just hope to see you all again soon.
Love to Father, Mother, brothers and sisters, my dar-
ling children and all our friends and acquaintances, the
aunts, uncles, nephews, nieces[,] *everyone*, lots of love

to Waldy, Sis, Jan, Henk and a big kiss to everyone.
Riek Mama[89]

But the war was playing a cruel game with the lives caught up in
the Nazi war machine. For just as a twist in fate had cost Rika and
Waldemar their guesthouse on the Seafront in 1942, the advance of the
liberating armies led to increasingly worse conditions for the prisoners.
Although his empire was crumbling, Adolf Hitler continued to frantically issue orders with one goal in mind: never surrender. His aim was
to prolong the war as long as he could so as to wipe as many Jews from
the face of the earth as possible. In Poland, the chimneys of the extermination camps were now smoking day and night, and people waited
in line for hours for the gas chamber; in the concentration camps, the
regime was becoming stricter by the day. At Vught, the Dutch Kapos
were replaced by hard criminals from the German camps, the Red Cross
packages and other privileges were cut, and the punishments became
increasingly severe.

The guards at Vught had panic in their eyes, and the women in the
barracks kept their ears open. In the distance did they hear the explosions of bridges being blown up to stop the Allies' advance? They most
certainly heard the firing squads in the men's camp, where four hundred
and fifty prisoners were executed at the end of the war. Meanwhile,
rumors were flying around in The Hague about impending large-scale
deportations from Vught to Germany, and in a smuggled letter, Rika's
sisters urgently advised her to fall from somewhere or to take some other
drastic measure that would land her in the hospital so that if the trains
did come, she wouldn't have to get on. A few days later, her sisters went
to the hospital near Vught in the hope of finding Rika there. But all
they found were a few fellow prisoners who had taken the same advice
to heart. As for Rika, she replied with her usual bravado: "They can go
right ahead, but I'm not about to do myself in for anybody."[90]

On August 30, another smuggled letter arrived in The Hague:

Vught, Wednesday p.m.

Dear Father, Mother, brothers & sisters, my dear sweet
children,

It's evening again and it's already getting dark. Just
got the package from Jo. I already wrote about the
other packages in my last letters. I'm writing to you
in bed because we are now under strict watch. So, I
don't dare to write during the day anymore. I always
thank God when the letter is gone. Everyone, please be
careful when writing. Always make sure that when the
letter changes hands, it won't bring harm to the people
trying to help us, understood! Because that would
make me even sadder. Never say a word about these
letters to anyone, you hear? Say you heard everything
from the folks who brought the message.

Dear darlings, I hope that we can come home
soon. I crave it. I don't think I will be home before the
war ends. It's been 8 months already—rough, huh?
But if Waldemar is doing okay, that's the main thing,
and that you all stay healthy, that's my greatest wish.
My spirit hasn't been broken yet. And I remember that
every day is one day closer to being home, and the
days are sometimes horrible, for you all don't know
what *Häftling* [prisoner] means. You are *nothing*, there
is *nothing* left of who you are. It is sometimes too
wonderful to think of being free and being able to hug
you all. And then I will see my sweet, good children
and my dear husband once again. My goodness, how I
yearn for *all of you!*

Hello to my dear brothers and sisters, hello to
Father and Mother, embraced by you all. Riek.[91]

On Sunday, September 3, 1944, the prisoners worked from seven in the morning to twelve noon as usual. But when they returned to their barracks, it became clear that this had been their last relatively normal day. The guards were hastily packing their bags, and the entire camp smelled of burning paper—the prisoners' files in flames. The radio had announced that Allied tanks were advancing through Belgium and now had the Dutch border in sight. In the days that followed, the prisoners gazed intently out at the horizon through the barbed wire: the liberating armies could appear at any moment, and finally, they'd all be able to go home. Two days later, Germans and members of the Dutch Nazi party all over the Netherlands took flight. In The Hague, Waldy and his buddies spent this *"Dolle Dinsdag,"* or Mad Tuesday, heckling the departing escapees from the Hoorn Bridge in Rijswijk. No one was cursing louder or dancing more wildly than Waldy. The madness was finally over, his parents would come home, and they could go back to the Seafront.

But while Waldy was enjoying the happiest moments of the war, long, empty cargo trains were rolling into Vught. The camp was completely evacuated within forty-eight minutes. Even the inventory from the camp hospital and the machines from the Philips workstations were loaded into the trains. Then, nearly thirty-five hundred prisoners were hastily boarded into the cars. They were given bread for three days. Among the last to board the train on the afternoon of September 6 were Rika and the remaining female prisoners.

Unlike their male counterparts, the women were allowed to take a few personal possessions with them. They were wearing their summer clothes—a light-blue uniform with a red cross on the back and headscarves with blue polka dots. No one thought to bring winter clothes, for surely the Dutch Resistance would sabotage the trains and set them free before they reached the German border. But that night, the trains thundered across the border in Zevenaar unhindered, leaving Holland behind. They were barreling toward an unknown destination—and the winter.

8

North-Northeast

For two days and two nights, the Vught women rode through darkened Germany. The train cars were overcrowded and suffocating, but still the male prisoners could hear the ladies singing over the chugging of the wheels. At the Sachsenhausen concentration camp in Oranienburg, the cars carrying the men were disconnected. Rika and the eight hundred women who shared her fate rode northward, following roughly the same route Waldemar had taken four months earlier: north-northeast. Midway through the morning of September 9, the train came to a halt in Fürstenberg, a tiny town in the vast forests of Brandenburg and Mecklenburg.

It was a beautiful late summer's day. Dressed in their blue jumpsuits, the Dutch women marched proudly across the majestic landscape under the watchful eyes of the SS guards. A couple miles in, they passed an idyllic lake surrounded by reeds billowing in the wind, which was known as the Schwedtsee. Some of the women picked flowers, hoping that they would brighten up their new barracks. They knew where they were going by then—Ravensbrück, the concentration camp set up by Himmler in 1938 for all the women who did not fit the Aryan

Kinder-Küche-Kirche ideal: criminals, prostitutes, Roma, and, in recent years, increasing numbers of Resistance fighters from all over Europe. One of the prisoners among them had already spent some time at Ravensbrück and assured them that it was quite clean and orderly. She told them how every morning they conducted a thorough check to make sure the prisoners had made their beds neatly.

A little while later, the Vught women entered the camp. Their first impression was already strange: behind the barbed wire were skinny, filthy women with arms stretched out and pleading looks on their faces. Unanimously, they decided to toss them the bread they had left over from the trip—it was stale anyway, and surely, they'd be getting fresh bread soon. But as soon as they arrived at the camp's main building, they were rounded up onto a sort of soot-covered mound and left to their own devices. It started to rain and eventually got cold, but they were given neither food nor shelter. When blankets were distributed that evening, they realized that they would have to spend the night out there, hungry.

The orderly women's camp of a few years prior no longer existed. Now that prisoners had been rounded up from every corner of the crumbling Third Reich and transported to the still seemingly "safe" camps in Schleswig-Holstein, Ravensbrück—which was already bursting at the seams after the emptying of the Polish ghettos—had fallen into complete chaos. The day after they arrived, the Dutch women were taken into a large tent and registered. Rika was assigned number 67001. They were sent to the showers, after which they had to trade in their tidy blue jumpsuits and headscarves for a pile of rags thrown to them by the German and Polish Kapos. A giant red cross was painted on the back of their clothes as a sign of their prisoner status. Some women didn't receive underwear. They were lodged in a barrack built for four hundred people, but which now housed more than twelve hundred. There were hardly any beds: three prisoners had to share a single cot and a straw sack. The place was extraordinarily filthy, and it wasn't long before the newcomers started violently scratching: the lice and fleas were all too eager to pounce on the fresh supply of flesh.

***

The news of the invasion of Western Europe, the course of the war, and the evacuation of the camps had reached Neuengamme as well. From his little post office, Waldemar frantically tried to find out what had happened to his wife:

September 10, 1944

> Dear Jo,
>
> Haven't heard anything from you in a long time.
>
> How is it going in Holland? You are all well, I hope. It must be a stressful time for you too. I'm worried about what happened to Riek. Whether she is staying there or being transferred.
>
> And Waldy, how are you my boy? Are you back in school again?
>
> Got a letter and a big package from Sis the day before yesterday, unfortunately the fruit had gone bad, but the other things were delicious. Thanks, Sis. Everything is fine here, only that it's cold and rains a lot. Otherwise, nothing new to report. I'm just waiting.
>
> Riek, the time is moving quickly and soon all this will be over. Sending my warmest greetings to all,
>
> Waldemar[92]

But Waldemar's words of comfort never reached Rika. At Vught, the prisoners had had plenty of opportunities to feel connected to their old lives, but at Ravensbrück they found themselves trapped on a sort of island, where all vital necessities were in short supply and where most prisoners had long since given up their humanity—a luxury that one simply couldn't afford under such circumstances. Only once were the Dutch women allowed to write a letter home from Ravensbrück, and only a small number of those letters ever reached their destination. And the prisoners received no mail whatsoever, let alone food packages or smuggled correspondence.

Because of their experience at Philips, most of the forced laborers from Vught were sent to work in the Siemens electronics factory. They lined up for roll call every morning at four o'clock; and at six o'clock, they marched single file to their workstations, where they worked for twelve hours nonstop. At the end of the work day, they stood for the equally long evening roll call and never returned to their barracks before eight o'clock at night.

Despite everything, the Vught women were relatively fit and well fed, and their morale was largely unaffected at first. Although they became increasingly spread out across the camp, their solidarity remained high. And solidarity was as good a survival strategy as any, because without friends no one would make it. Rika shared her love and sorrow with a young concert pianist and her mother, both of whom had been in the Resistance in The Hague, and with a nurse from the Zaandam area who had worked as a courier. They comforted each other even as the daily misery, filth, lice, hunger, and illnesses threatened to over-power them. They distracted themselves with songs and little skits and kept each other going with optimistic scenarios: Siemens was building a new barrack—surely the conditions would be better there; Queen Wilhelmina was supposedly already back on Dutch soil—the liberation of Europe couldn't be far off now. And in all the terrifying chaos, one thing seemed certain: the German Empire was collapsing—it couldn't last much longer. Surely, they'd be home by Christmas.

On November 1, Rika celebrated All Saints' Day with an impro-vised yet well-attended mass in the delousing tent. In circumstances that brought out the most godless side of humanity, faith had become, for Rika and many others, more important than ever. But weeks went by, the days were getting colder, and still they weren't free. After a while despair started setting in, especially after the first vigils were held for friends who had succumbed to one of the many infectious diseases rampant in the filthy barracks. The final blow came in early December, when a Polish woman who had previously been in Auschwitz told them what was happening there.

Most of the Vught women came from an educated background. They read the newspaper, had been quick to recognize the dangers of fascism, and had earned their spurs in the Resistance. But they had always assumed that they were risking their freedom to save Jewish people from hard labor camps—even the most cynical among them would never have imagined that the Germans, even with all their ideological nonsense, would have been capable of such a deliberate and large-scale annihilation of innocent people. The realization devastated them; one after the other, they started to break down—physically, but even more so in terms of morale.

Over time, the young and strong usually managed to recover. They banished every thought of the past and future from their minds and focused on one thing—survival—from hour to hour, day to day, without ever doubting they'd pull through: "Giving in is giving up." But some abandoned hope, and with it their life force. In mid-December, the pianist's mother, with whom Rika had developed a close friendship, died. At fifty-three years old, Rika was now the oldest in their group, but her spirit hadn't been broken. She remained, as a fellow prisoner would later recount, "immensely cheerful." With the same nearly desperate optimism that had carried her through so much misery in the early 1930s, she now clung to hope for a quick and happy end and a safe return to her children and her two Waldys.

Meanwhile, Rika's family in The Hague waited in vain for news about their oldest daughter and sister. But all that arrived was a letter

addressed to Rika from a former cellmate in Scheveningen who had also
been with her at Vught. Even she had been set free by then, and she
clearly assumed that "Aunt Riek" had been released as well:

> I was shocked when I was suddenly greeted by you and
> Aunt Lena in Vught; I had thought you were already
> free. I was so incredibly happy to receive your con-
> gratulations and the chocolates. That was a truly sweet
> idea of yours. Is it true that your husband was trans-
> ferred to Germany? How terrible that must be for you.
> And how is little Waldy? He must have been so thrilled
> to have his mother come home. Fortunately, you still
> have him. And your other family has surely been very
> dear to you in these difficult times. I still remember
> all the letters you got in the cell and how they sympa-
> thized with everything.
>
> The war is lasting forever, isn't it? Do you remem-
> ber how back in February we expected the end every
> day with Wil and Ria? Now here we are, almost a year
> later. But I don't let it get me down. *Keep smiling*, right!
> I still laugh. We have to stay just as strong when the
> men come home. And what a day that will be! That's
> something we can really long for! We never would have
> thought that everything would be so horrible, but I'm
> even more amazed by the fact that people can endure so
> much. You get knocked down again and again, and you
> stand back up and keep going. Will we ever know truly
> happy times again, Aunt Riek? Yes, despite everything,
> I'm still sure of it, and that's what keeps me going.[93]

In mid-December 1944, Hitler launched the Ardennes Counteroffensive, later known as the Battle of the Bulge. It was a campaign

doomed to fail, just like the bloody, human-life-devouring, last-ditch attempt that had cost the German armies their momentum on the Eastern Front. But the counteroffensive brought the Allies' advance to a halt, the war was put on hold, and the prisoners in the concentration camps were still not home by Christmas. They held secret Christmas services above the barracks, where they could hear the flocks of geese honking to each other overhead so as not to get lost in the fog. But for all the people who had been scattered around ravaged Europe, all efforts to communicate with the outside world were in vain—by the last winter of the war, all postal lines had been cut off.

***

Neither Ravensbrück nor Neuengamme was designed to exterminate people. The concentration camps were built in a time when the Third Reich was running like a well-oiled machine, and the goal was to punish people, reeducate them in the Nazi ideology, and use their labor to benefit the empire's growth. It was a time when vision, order, and clarity were among the most attractive qualities of National Socialism, making it appealing to people with a strong sense of duty, people who would rather blame their actions on a system than have to take responsibility themselves. But in the winter months of 1945, the Nazi empire found itself in the throes of death, lethally wounded and thrashing its giant claws around in an attempt to ward off attacks from all sides. The brain had gone insane, but the limbs were still trying to carry out the tasks they had once been intended for.

And so, the trains were still running off and on, and prisoners were still being transferred by the thousands from the occupied territories to northern Germany's concentration camps. In furious attempts to make use of the fresh supply of labor, the Nazis continued to establish new subcamps, only to abandon them again. The big, unwieldy machine that had swallowed Waldemar and Rika alive faltered, held fast, and churned on as furiously as ever, even though there was nothing more to be gained. The enormous army of weak and hungry prisoners was nothing more than dead weight for the doomed empire, and their labor did nothing but postpone the end of a pointless war.

Hitler's pseudo-Darwinist theories about the Aryan people's need to fight for Lebensraum were now being manifested daily in the camp in the most atrocious ways imaginable. People were dying not because of the Nazis' sadism or their desire to murder individuals per se but in a battle for survival in a world where there simply wasn't enough to go around. Order had deteriorated into chaos, and the people who had been running the camps for years with discipline lost all control. Some turned to drinking or other forms of excess as a means of escape, while others suppressed their fear by resorting to even crueler methods of keeping the prisoners in line. Executions and abuse escalated. In the end, even those who managed to hold on to their humanity could do little to help the prisoners who were being crushed in the Third Reich's fight to the death.

Although Neuengamme was still reasonably well organized compared to Ravensbrück, its living conditions began to deteriorate dramatically in the fall of 1944 as well. There were around fourteen hundred people living in the main camp. Soup was still being served, but the ladlefuls were getting smaller by the day. Blankets were still available, but not everyone got one. The showers were still running, but prisoners hardly ever got to take one and were eventually deprived of them altogether. And then there was the cold. Winter set in early and with a vengeance, and during roll call, they often stood for hours up to their knees in snow. In many cases, the newcomers were so paralyzed by the situation that many of them didn't survive more than a few weeks, and there were so many deaths that the SS deemed it necessary to build a second crematorium on-site.

Camp veterans like Waldemar had a better chance of survival. They understood the camp's underlying structure and its unwritten rules, and their morale was strengthened by the mere fact that, thanks to their position, they were more than a face in the camp's anonymous masses. For Waldemar, the camp's general filthiness was abhorrent, and he'd never had a high tolerance for the cold, but he had inherited his father's tough constitution and was still in reasonably good shape. The worst part for him was the fact that he hadn't received any news from Holland or Rika in months. In a letter sent to the Netherlands on January 7, 1945, his despair seems to creep between the lines:

> Dear Jo,
>   First of all, a happy new year 1945 to you, Mother, Father and everyone. Everything's well at home, I hope. Have you heard anything from Rika? If so, please don't forget to send me her address, number, and camp, so I can write to her. It's depressing to not receive any letters at all.
>   And Waldy, my boy, how are you? Work hard and do your best in football. And Jo, you must have also had a hard time under the current circumstances. I'm doing fine and fortunately, I'm healthy. It can get extremely cold here, but I'm coping. Please write back as soon as possible. You too, Waldy, I'm waiting.
>   Greetings to everyone, especially Jo.
>   So long, your Waldemar[94]

Five days later, the Soviet troops dealt a major blow to the Eastern Front. Hundreds of thousands of citizens fled. By then, most of Germany, from children to old men, had joined the fight. They believed they were giving their lives for victory, but in fact they were in a battle for ultimate destruction, a battle that their dictator, isolated under four meters of armed concrete in his Berlin bunker, had chosen over all forms of surrender.

Occasionally, a scrap of news would make it out of the concentration camps and find its way to Holland. That's how, after several anxious months without news, the Chardon family finally learned on February 11 what had happened to their Kees, who had been transferred from Vught to Germany as well. An escaped prisoner had met him by chance in one of Neuengamme's subcamps, where he had apparently been transferred from the Heinkel factory in Sachsenhausen. Elated, Kees's sister in Delft wrote in her diary:

> He worked in a village near Helmstedt (Morsleben?)
> between Hanover and Magdeburg. The food was good
> and no trouble with bombings. Maybe, just maybe,
> word from Kees himself will make it through from
> there. At least we know where he is now. The Russians
> are close. He will be home before we know it![95]

But meanwhile, she had no idea that, according to his fellow prisoners, her brother, with his small frame, had very little chance of survival in the salt mines in Helmstedt. "It was evident that he was neither psychologically nor physically fit for life in the camp," as one of them later wrote.[96] Nevertheless, Kees endured it surprisingly well at first. Like Rika, he held on to his deep-rooted faith, and like her, he had a close-knit group of friends from his Vught days around him for support. Only when his best friend finally succumbed to the hardship at the end of February did his spirit finally break. For days, he didn't work or eat, and he wandered around the camp with vacant eyes. Even the harshest guards left him alone. "He seemed to have lost his will to survive," said one of his fellow prisoners later.

***

At the end of the summer of 1944, pressing letters were sent to Berlin about the growing abuse in the concentration camps. The reply of the

Nazi elites was consistent with the simple, ruthless ideas that formed the basis of their entire ideology: the weak must disappear to make room for the strong. In September, Himmler ordered a gas chamber to be built in Ravensbrück. That fall, the building was constructed on the Schwedtsee, right next to the camp's crematorium, and in Uckermark, located just outside of the main camp, a hospital was set up. Previously, this subcamp had served as a division for underage girls, and thus became known as the *Jugendlager*, the youth camp.

That December, the gas chambers were put into use. Originally, they were intended for hopeless hospital patients, who up until then had been killed via poison injections, but the chaos had gotten so out of hand that it was soon decided that the "natural" death rate needed to be accelerated. That winter, selections were made every day at four o'clock in the work barracks: anyone who appeared too sick, too weak, or too old to work was sent either to *"Mitwerda,"* as the gas chamber was called in campspeak, or to the Jugendlager. The latter was nothing more than a delayed execution, for prisoners sent to the Jugendlager were given hardly anything to eat, and there were no blankets or medical services to speak of. At the end of the day, the Kapos dragged the dead to the crematorium and the most miserable cases to the gas chamber, or—if there wasn't enough room—to the trucks reconstructed for gassing purposes. The bodies were burned, and the ashes were dumped into the waters of the Schwedtsee. Only the very few who managed to recover on their own strength had any chance of making it out of the Jugendlager alive. They were allowed to return to the normal barracks.

It wasn't long before the entire camp realized that being selected for the Jugendlager was something to be avoided at all costs. When it came time for selection, they did everything they could to make even the sick look as healthy as possible. The women pinched each other's cheeks, smeared blood to add color to the skin if necessary, and secretly propped up anyone who was truly no longer able to stand. But in February, when daytime temperatures barely climbed above twenty degrees below freezing, the snow was more than three feet deep, and the Baltic Sea was practically frozen solid, a dysentery epidemic broke out in Rika's barrack. This exceptionally infectious intestinal disease ravaged its victims in weeks, eating away both their bodies and minds.

On a cold day at the end of the month, eighty more women were selected for the Jugendlager. Among the dirty, emaciated souls who, with the casual flick of a finger were sent staggering to the dreaded hospital, was number 67001, the woman who in another life had been Rika Nods, wife of Waldemar, mother of Waldy. A few weeks later, twenty of these women managed to make such a healthy impression that they were sent back to the main camp. Rika wasn't one of them.

***

A couple hundred miles to the west, Waldemar was still hanging on—filthy, hungry, and colder than he ever could have thought possible in his life. After the postal lines were cut off, the post office was discontinued, and Waldemar was transferred to an administrative position in the camp's weaving division. He was moved to Barrack 4, which was still one of the better ones. His compatriot and fellow ocean swimmer Anton de Kom, the man who had once preached from the De Waag balcony on Paramaribo's Waterfront, hadn't been so lucky, however. He had been arrested in August 1944 for his activities with the underground press and transferred from Sachsenhausen to Neuengamme at the start of the year. And even though he and Waldy looked so much alike that they were often mistaken for each other—both were tall and thin, and in the absence of hygiene, both had grown a wild head of hair—De Kom had arrived during a period when the SS guards no longer had any time to amuse themselves with a black man. Thus, he'd been forced to join the regular masses.

But De Kom didn't have to worry about being transferred to one of the dreaded subcamps: people of color were not allowed to leave the camp under any circumstances for fear that they might escape and rape

German women, thereby soiling the Aryan race with their blood. Fellow prisoners would later recall how he, even in the camp, continued to tell stories about the balmy, enchanting beauty of his *Switi Sranan*. But not Waldemar. Imprisoned on a continent that wasn't his own, caught up in a war he had nothing to do with, he could no longer remember the colors of his homeland. His memories of Suriname, which after years in rigid Holland had already grown dim, all but disappeared behind the German barbed wire.

The Red Armies were advancing in the East, and millions of citizens, collaborators, and soldiers were being driven out and pushed toward Berlin. Meanwhile, the Allied bombers had virtually free rein of the skies and were dropping an inferno of fire and explosions on one German city after another. The Third Reich was up in flames, but total devastation wasn't enough for Hitler. On March 19, 1945, he issued the so-called Nero Decree, which called for the destruction of railroads, factories, and other fundamental facilities in Germany. April came, and the chaos increased. The British tanks arrived at the Elbe, and one order was contradicted by the next. Prisoners were shuffled back and forth, either in open cattle cars or on foot, usually without food or water, and they were constantly bombarded by the Allied planes swarming Germany like flies in search of enemy soldiers on the move.

Still, musical performances and sports matches were organized on Sunday afternoons in Neuengamme's central square. Only now there were the ominous silhouettes of dead bodies hanging from the gallows in the background. As it became more difficult to maintain order in the catastrophically overcrowded camp, and clear that the whole system was on the verge of collapse, the Kapos and SS guards became increasingly barbaric. Some spent the final days of their supposedly eternal empire in a drunken stupor, while others took pleasure in exercising their tyranny one last time. Still others tried to cozy up to the influential prisoners, in the hope that they'd receive preferential treatment after the war.

In mid-April, around three thousand prisoners were brought from Camp Helmstedt to the makeshift Camp Wöbbelin near Ludwigslust. The guards were thrown into such a panic that they fled en masse, leaving the exhausted, half-starved, and in some cases, dying prisoners to their fate. On April 16, Kees Chardon, the small man with the tremendous spirit, passed away. Together with his last surviving friend, he had managed, against all odds, to stay alive for months. A few hours after he died, his friend passed away as well.

Their bodies were found a few weeks later by American soldiers, who were so shocked by what they found in the camp that they forced the local villagers to walk through it themselves, so they could see with their own eyes what had been going on in their backyard. But no matter what Kees Chardon had been forced to endure in the camps, the Nazis never made a beast out of him. As a French survivor wrote:

> Oddly enough, he remained soft in an environment where there was no softness to speak of. He managed, through his unique dignity, to resist the ultimate villain. He commanded respect, and one couldn't scare him. He gave his life so as not [to] lose his humanity, without any concessions whatsoever.[97]

On April 19, the Nazis' evacuation of Neuengamme began. Outside the camp the birds were singing the arrival of spring, but inside a feverish commotion had taken over. Thousands of prisoners were marched out the gate and into the cargo trains, while behind them, in the blazing fires of the cremation ovens, were the bodies of the silent witnesses: Jewish children used for medical experiments, Communists hung by order of the Hamburg Gestapo—all thrown in with the remains of the slaughtered bloodhounds. Finally, the gallows were sawed into pieces and fed to the flames. Meanwhile, in the offices next to the SS building, administrative employees were erasing all information related to punishment procedures from the camp's files; but this quickly became too time consuming, and hundreds of folders were tossed into the ovens at once.

The Nazis clung to their prisoners like, as historian Jacques Presser would later write, a wounded predator that had sunk its teeth into its prey. Cargo trains continued to arrive daily and were then transferred to other camps. Anton de Kom ended up in the subcamp of Sandbostel, where he died of hunger and exhaustion on April 24. But most of the prisoners were sent north, to the sea, the only direction the SS could go now that the Allied troops were making an unstoppable advance from the south.

Within a week and a half, the main camp was totally dismantled. The last train departed on April 29 carrying the seven hundred prisoners who had been deployed for the evacuation and kept behind to cover up their tracks. Waldemar was among them. The Neuengamme concentration camp had officially ceased to exist. The ovens were still warm, but there was nothing left in the empty barracks but the whispering of lost souls.

Partially on foot, partially via the still-functioning rail lines, the prisoners were driven toward the port city of Lübeck on the Baltic Sea, almost forty miles north of Hamburg. As pleased as they were to see the devastation the Allied bombers had caused, they lived in constant fear of being attacked by the Tommies flying over the Third Reich in search of prey. When they arrived at the coast, they were boarded onto cargo ships. In the vessels' dark holds, which were not the least bit suitable for human transport, the prisoners found themselves in a battle of life and death over a bread crumb or a drop of water.

Starting on April 26, the early shipment of prisoners was boarded onto the *Cap Arcona*, a majestic ocean steamer anchored about two and a half miles from the shore. When it was first launched in 1927, the *Cap Arcona* was fully equipped with electricity, propelled by twenty-four thousand horsepower and staffed with at least eighty-four cooks, making it one of the most luxurious steamers of its time. It was "the queen of the Hamburg-South America line." In 1942 it was mobilized as a floating base for the German Kriegsmarine in Gotenhafen and used by propaganda minister Joseph Goebbels as the set of a movie about the *Titanic*. However, the film never made it to the silver screen because the violent evacuation scenes were considered too heavy for the already-demoralized German people. During the final months of the war, the ship, which had since been painted gray, was used to rescue German citizens and soldiers from areas threatened by the Red Army. The vessel had already taken more than twenty-six thousand refugees across the Baltic Sea to safety.

Now the weathered, yet ever-luxurious *Cap Arcona* was host to thousands of broken, skittish prisoners. For the men, it was like ascending straight to heaven from hell. They ran their bony fingers across the sofas, silk-covered walls, marble chimneys, and lemonwood tables. They stretched out on the soft mattresses in the cabins and marveled at the hot and cold running water. There were even stewards on board who politely requested that they take care not to damage or dirty the furniture. The biggest shock of all, however, came in the dining room. There, standing under the crystal chandeliers, they stared at themselves in the full-length mirrors. Most of them hadn't seen themselves in years and didn't recognize themselves anymore. They had become ghosts.

Meanwhile, what the Germans had hoped to achieve by boarding the concentration camp prisoners onto the *Cap Arcona* and the other smaller vessels anchored in the Bay of Lübeck was entirely unclear. Optimists suggested that in a humane gesture, Himmler had decided to send them to neutral Sweden, but others believed the decision was a variation of "Measure X," which the Nazis had carried out a few weeks earlier: rather than allowing the prisoners to fall into enemy hands, the camps were blown up with everything and everyone inside. Likewise, if the ships were to sink offshore, thousands of witnesses to the regime's crimes would disappear all at once to the bottom of the sea.

On May 1 a rumor spread around the ship like wildfire: Hitler was dead. Officially, he had fallen "in the final battle against Bolshevism," but in fact, he had committed suicide together with his mistress, Eva Braun, in his Berlin bunker on April 30. In his last will and testament, he left the remainder of the Third Reich to navy admiral Karl Dönitz. In an effort to save what little was left to be saved for the German people, Dönitz postponed the Nazis' inevitable surrender to allow as many soldiers to return home from the war zones as possible. Meanwhile, the captain of the *Cap Arcona* tried to convince the SS commander on duty to let him take the ship into the harbor in Lübeck, and the underground camp leadership made frantic attempts to establish contact with the approaching liberators. The first Allied reconnaissance planes had been spotted circling above the bay, and it was not yet certain whether they knew that the *Cap Arcona* and the small ships around it were in fact a floating concentration camp.

However, the days that followed were calm. There was little to eat on board, but the six hundred crew members and sailors did what they could to help their unusual cargo recover from their hardships and to protect them from the SS guards on board. The weather was pleasant, and the prisoners basked in the sun on the decks. Waldemar was able to look out at the horizon for the first time in years—the same horizon he had looked at from the house on the Seafront. Across the bay was the green, steeple-dotted coastline of northern Germany, and between the trees were the shimmering seaside resorts that, in peacetime, had made the shores of the Baltic Sea such a delightful place to be.

May 3 arrived. Grand Admiral Dönitz negotiated the conditions for a total surrender with Field Marshal Montgomery, and on the *Cap Arcona* the prisoners could already hear the sound of British artillery on land. Small boats traveled back and forth between the ships and the shore, and the atmosphere was almost festive. It was a beautiful day, a day to be free.

9

The Cuckoo in the Nest

A few weeks after the liberation on May 5, while the Netherlands was still flushed with victory, Waldy had a dream about his parents. He was riding in the tram through The Hague, and all of a sudden, he saw them sitting together happily on a bench. They looked exactly as they had when he last saw them in the hallway of the police station on the Javastraat. He called out to them with joy and tried to push his way through the other passengers to reach them, but for some reason his legs refused to cooperate, and no matter how much he shouted and waved, he couldn't get their attention. They looked past him as if he didn't exist. And that's when he knew.

In the year and a half since the Pijnboomstraat raid, Waldy had made his own journey north-northeast. After six months at his grandparents' house, he had to leave. They were old, and the economic crisis of the 1930s had cost them much of their former wealth—they simply couldn't accommodate the needs of a lively, growing boy. When, after Mad Tuesday, it became clear that the war still wasn't over yet, he moved in with Aunt Jo, who, of all his aunts, had always been his favorite. But money was hard to come by in her house as well, and when food

became scarcer and more expensive that fall, Waldy was sent to live with
Aunt Mien, the most well-off of all the sisters. But clearly, she too was
ill prepared to take in a restless fifteen-year-old. Therefore, when the
opportunity to send city children to the countryside presented itself in
January 1945, the Van der Lans family was grateful to take advantage
of it.

Together with forty other boys, Waldy was taken by truck to the
northern Dutch town of Hoogkarspel. There, too, he was transferred
from one family to another—most likely it hadn't occurred to everyone
in the village that a soft-skinned city kid could also happen to be the
first black boy they'd ever seen. Finally, he was lovingly welcomed into
a large, hospitable farm family. It was there that he, already a lanky
adolescent, celebrated the Netherlands' liberation on May 5, 1945. And
there, in the days and weeks that followed, he waited for his parents to
come walking down the garden path, and for the day the three of them
would be together again. No one seemed to have any doubts about
the fact that his parents were coming home. As his aunts always said:
"Your mother is so strong, so optimistic—there's no way they could
break her"; and his father was such a young, athletic man—he had said
himself in his letters that he was coping with camp life.

But no one came. No telegram, no phone call, no word whatsoever—
nothing. After a few weeks, Marcel and Jan van der Lans decided to go
to Germany to pick up their sister themselves. But in the barracks on
the Schwedtsee all they found were German prisoners of war guarded
by the Russian soldiers who had liberated Ravensbrück at the end of
April. The camp was mostly empty by the time they arrived, because in
the weeks after Germany capitulated, all the prisoners left standing had
been packed into cargo trains and sent to God knows where.

After coming home to Holland empty-handed, Marcel put out an
ad in all the national newspapers and several local ones:

Who can provide me with information about **Mrs. Rika Nods-v.d.Lans**, b. in The Hague, 29-9-91. Taken captive in Jan. '44, in Scheveningen prison until May '44, at Vught until Sept '44, number 0988, later transferred to Ravensbrück (Ger.), no news since then. Also looking for **Waldemar Nods** (West-Indian), b. 1 Sept. 1908 in Paramaribo. Taken captive in Jan '44, in Scheveningen prison until Feb '44, at Vught until Jun '44, later transferred to Neuengamme (Ger.), number 32180, worked in the post office. Last heard from him in Jan. '45. Visits or letters most welcome, naturally, all costs will be reimbursed.[98]

The ad was also read aloud on a radio program specifically dedicated to that purpose, *Radiobaken* on Radio Herrijzend Nederland. Finally, the family received a reply: a short letter from someone who had been in hiding on the Stevinstraat and was now looking for the bed frame and down-filled duvets he had left there. Marcel had seen enough in Germany to be realistic: for every day that went by with no news, the chances of his sister and brother-in-law coming home alive grew slimmer.

On June 28, Waldy went to the Petrolea building in The Hague to submit an official request for information about his parents at the Dutch Red Cross. In his schoolboy's handwriting, he filled in the form about his mother: "From Vught transferred to Ravelsbroek [sic]," next to which a civil servant later wrote: "Probably sent to Sweden."[99] But the glimmer of hope quickly faded when the Dutch embassy in Sweden confirmed with certainty that Hendrika J. M. Nods-van der Lans was not among the female prisoners who had been rescued from collapsing Germany in the final weeks of the war.

Still, the Dutch diplomats inquired about her among the former prisoners recovering in the Swedish countryside. In early July, someone came forth claiming that she had indeed known someone called "Aunt

Riek," but as far as she knew, this woman had died. While the Red
Cross was attempting to follow up on this lead with other survivors, a
second answer to Marcel's ad arrived on July 12. The letter was from the
young pianist with whom Rika had developed such a close friendship in
the camp. She had been boarded onto a train right after being selected
for the Jugendlager herself. She was rescued by a Swedish diplomat,
more dead than alive, and only now was she well enough to travel back
to Holland.

A few days later, Waldy was helping his host family with the potato
harvest when he saw his foster mother making her way across the field
with one of her daughters. She had tears in her eyes and a letter in her
hand.

> Dear Waldy,
>
> You have probably heard the upsetting news from
> the Ooteman family that your dear Mother and our
> dear sister will not be coming home. It is terrible. How
> we have all longed for her, and you will surely miss her
> more than anyone. We talked to someone—we put out
> ads—who told us that she was transferred in February
> to the Knitting Department of the Jugendlager in
> Ravensbrück along with around 80 other women. In
> early March, about 20 of them came back, the others
> had died of dysentery. The young woman was sure, she
> recognized us immediately because Aunt Bertha and I
> look so much like your mother. She will ask the other
> survivors in Sweden to send us more information.
>
> I hope that you will never forget your mother in
> your prayers. It must have been so horrible for her to
> die alone in a strange place. Oh, how she must have
> longed to be with her children. Remember, Waldy, to

pray for your mother earnestly and often, for she surely passed without any spiritual assistance.

We have heard that there is still hope for your father. Several prisoners were taken to Ludwigslust or Porta Westfalica in March. These areas were liberated by the Russians, or that's what we heard from a doctor who had known your father there. He claims that it was impossible to send any letters from there, so we shouldn't give up hope quite yet. Waldy, I wish you strength with all my heart and urgently ask again that you not forget your mother in your prayers. God will surely have mercy upon her!

Your Aunt Jo[100]

In Groningen, Willem Hagenaar cried when he heard that his former wife and the love of his life had lost her final battle with fate. "It never should have happened this way," he said over and over again. "It never should have happened this way." A year later, he finally married Jans, the quiet village girl who had lived and loved for all those years in the shadow of her impressive predecessor.

Waldy couldn't cry. In the weeks after Jo's letter, he buried himself in his work in the countryside. It was as if he already knew, he later thought. July and August went by, and in The Hague, Marcel did his best to take care of his late sister's affairs. He had nearly given up all hope of his brother-in-law's return. "I haven't heard anything about Waldemar, only a vague message that he could be sick. But if I can be honest, I am convinced that he is dead too," he wrote to his brother.[101] He gathered information about potentially suitable boarding schools and spoke with David Millar in the hope that he would consider adopting his nephew into his family. Neither option worked out, and when Waldy returned to The Hague in September to redo his second year of high school, there was a large room reserved for him at his grandparents' house. It was furnished with his parents' sofa and a few other things that had been divided up among family members when the house on the Seafront was emptied, so that Waldy might feel a little more at home.

A little while later, a solemn requiem for Rika was held at Saint Anthony Abbot Church. The sanctuary was draped in black and everyone was in tears; everyone except Waldy. As he would later describe it, he just sat there brooding:

> If they had died in a normal manner, I would have
> had to attend two funerals, and there would have been
> a casket at the front of the church with my mother's
> body in it, I thought. But fortunately, that wasn't the
> case, otherwise I would have had to walk up to it.
> Still it was a shame, because Mama would have loved
> to have had flowers on her grave. She once said that
> she wanted to be buried in the churchyard on the
> Kerkhoflaan. Papa only wanted a stone. "No way,
> that's too cold and heavy," she would have said. Where
> are they lying now?[102]

But his thoughts were preoccupied with the Bible verses that the family had selected for Rika's prayer card. The one on the front he considered somewhat acceptable—"Greater love hath no man than this, that a man lay down his life for his friends"—but the one on the back was such a clear reference to his mother's supposedly sinful life that he swore off Catholicism then and there forever:

> I will arise and go to my Father, and will say unto him,
> Father, I have sinned against heaven, and before thee,
> and am no more worthy to be called thy son: make
> me as one of thy hired servants. But the Father said let

us eat and be merry: For this my son was dead, and is
alive again; he was lost, and is found. (Luke 15:18–24)
He that is without sin among you, let him first
cast a stone at her. (John 8:7)
Judge not, and ye shall not be judged. (Luke 6:37)[103]

Meanwhile, Marcel van der Lans made one last attempt to find out
what had happened to Waldy's father. He sent out a request for information to twenty-five people who, according to the Red Cross report,
had returned home from Neuengamme. Slowly, their replies trickled
in, some of them on recycled stationery because survivors received so
many of these sad inquiries. Most of them began with "To my deepest
regret . . . ," though there were a few who tried to offer a bit of hope:
There may still be some Dutch people in Russia—perhaps Mr. Nods is
there? But others implied that, given that five months had passed since
the liberation, there was very little chance that he was still alive. Perhaps,
they wrote, Mr. Van der Lans had heard about the terrible May 3 naval
disaster involving the *Cap Arcona* that had taken the lives of thousands
of prisoners from the Neuengamme camp.

On October 10, a telegram arrived from Waldy's aunt Hilda and
uncle Jo. Both had survived the Japanese POW camps: "Safe in British
hands hope to be home soon," they wrote.[104] When Waldy arrived home
from school a few days later, his old grandma greeted him with tears
in her eyes. She hugged him and said that he had to be strong, because
they had just received a letter from someone who had known his father
and was certain he had seen him on that ill-fated ship in the Baltic
Sea in early May. They could now safely assume that Waldemar was
never coming home. Waldy ran upstairs to his bedroom, but a few
minutes later he rushed back down, a cigarette in hand and—much to
his grandparents' bewilderment—whistling a happy tune. He bottled
up his tears and upheld the scouts' motto: "a scout whistles under all

circumstances." His grandfather was quick to scold him: How could he be so heartless?

The next day, Red Cross file number 7991—W. H. Nods was closed. There was no memorial service, but there was a short announcement in the *Haagsche Courant* newspaper, inconspicuously placed among dozens of similar messages.

> Following the previous notification from the Red Cross that Mrs. **Hendrika Nods-van der Lans** died in the "Ravensbrück" concentration camp, the Red Cross has recently confirmed that her husband, Mr. **Waldemar Nods**, last imprisoned in the "Neuengamme" concentration camp has died in the "Cap Arcona" disaster. On behalf of the family: M. J. H. van der Lans, Rotterdam, Statensingel 93-c.

In the East Indies, Hilda mourned the death of her favorite little brother, and on the other side of the world, an old man received word of the death of his youngest son, whom he had last seen on the Waterfront docks in Paramaribo more than twenty years ago. Koos Nods was almost eighty by then and still the same old sly fox he had always been. But once again he had lost his fortune, and months later Rika's family received a letter from the Brazilian jungle in which he claimed that he was first in line to the fortune that his promising young Waldemar had undoubtedly left behind in the wealthy Netherlands.

***

The exact circumstances of Rika and Waldemar's deaths were never completely clear, though the Van der Lans family would still try to find witnesses to their deaths in the 1970s. For his seventeenth birthday in 1946, Waldemar's grandparents gave him copies of the first publications in which concentration camp survivors recounted their horrifying memories. Despite their good intentions, the booklets brought him nothing but nightmares about gas chambers, sadistic guards, and burning ships. He remained particularly preoccupied with his father's death. How could that ship have been lost in the Bay of Lübeck so shortly before the end of the war? And how could such an excellent long-distance swimmer as his father have simply drowned?

Waldy's parents had disappeared without a trace, along with the millions of other people who never returned home from the East. In the first year after the end of the Second World War, the world gradually realized that something inconceivable had happened in Nazi Germany. It appeared that in total, more than six million Jews had been murdered. Of the 140,000 Jews living in the Netherlands before the war, only 34,000 survived; of the 11,000 that were rounded up in The Hague, only 500 returned. Only the Surinamese Jews had managed to escape unscathed: for once, their flexible views toward marriage and lack of precise registration in their country of origin had worked to their advantage.

The numbers from the "typical" German concentration camps were shocking in and of themselves. Of the approximately 132,000 registered prisoners at Ravensbrück, only 42,000 survived; of the 100,000 forced laborers at Neuengamme, barely half made it out alive. The massive slaughter in the men's camp mostly took place at the end of the war, during transport and the tragedy in the Bay of Lübeck.

The Chardon group was almost entirely wiped out: the florist and policeman with whom Kees had worked both died, the former in Neuengamme and the latter by firing squad on the Waalsdorpervlakte. Most of the "sheep" they had tried to save didn't survive the war either. Those who weren't immediately sent to the gas chambers in Auschwitz on February 11, 1944, died of either illness or exhaustion in the labor camps. Herman de Bruin, the medical student Rika and Waldemar had housed on the upper floor with Dobbe Franken, held out the longest—he died on March 28, 1945, in Dachau, more than a year after he was arrested. The residents of the Pijnboomstraat found their final resting places in the Red Cross archive in The Hague, in the endless rows of brown envelopes that made up the only tangible evidence of all the lives that were lost. Rika and Waldemar's envelopes were quite thick, a sign that there had been a considerable number of inquiries about their cases. Herman de Bruin's, on the other hand, was nearly empty: by the end of the war, there was simply no one left in his family to look for him.

The only one who had been able to mourn the once-so-promising medical student was the red-haired girl he had planned to spend his life with. Dobbe Franken survived forced labor, transport, diseases, and a total of five selections. On May 8, 1945, her camp in Czechoslovakia was liberated by the Russians, and she was one of the first Holocaust survivors to set foot on Dutch ground at the end of May 1945. At the crisis center in Eindhoven, she came across an old acquaintance who happened to have been with her Herman when he died. She was heartbroken, but thankful to have found out what happened to him so quickly. She was able to move on with her life, while others waited for years for news of loved ones whose cases were never truly closed. In 1946, she married a Jewish man from Poland who had served as a volunteer in the British army. Together they immigrated to Palestine, where Dobbe worked as a social worker and helped with the construction of Israel, the Jewish state founded to ensure there could never be another Holocaust.

In the summer of 1945, another survivor from the Pijnboomstraat returned to Holland virtually unharmed: Gerard van Haringen, the deserter SS man who had lived so comfortably with the Nods family. Back then, Rika had read his tarot cards and predicted that he would survive the war, and in his case, she had been right. He had managed to dodge the bullet intended for deserters and followed the same path as his host family. First, he was sent to Scheveningen and then to Vught, and finally he ended up in Germany at Dachau. His greatest fortune, he later described, was the fact that, unlike most of his fellow prisoners, he didn't have a family or lover to worry about. All he had to do was survive, and survive he did. Armed with his iron physique and knowledge of German, he managed, time and again, to secure the good jobs in the camps. He spent his time at Dachau washing the officers' cars, who in return shared their cigarettes and food with him. He was one of the few who could later look back and say that he had hardly ever been hungry in the camp.

After the camp was liberated, Gerard worked as an interpreter for the Americans for a few months and then decided to return home. This was easier said than done, for the Allies were extremely eager to catch former SS men in civilian clothes trying to avoid trial. But even though Gerard had never been particularly clever in school, he had been smart enough to avoid the mandatory SS tattoo under his left arm during his short period of service and was therefore able to slip through all the checkpoints without any problems. When he got home, his father was waiting for him at the train station in Rotterdam. He took his son in his arms and said: "Tomorrow you're going to turn yourself in."

But in the end, there was nothing to charge Gerard van Haringen with, other than his rash decision to join the SS, and he was released after a few months. A year and a half later, his case was dismissed. The judge decided that his time in Dachau had been punishment enough, and he didn't even lose his civil rights. Gerard, the survivor, had slipped through every loophole.

**

In Suriname, the war was—as the locals put it—fêted rather than fought. For once, the tables had been turned. Suddenly, they were the ones sending ships full of relief items to a plundered, impoverished Holland, rather than the other way around. The colony had prospered under American occupation, and the many dollars that had been exchanged for bauxite were now circulating in the Surinamese economy. A new sense of self-awareness had taken root within the population, which decades later would lead to a definitive separation from the motherland.

By the spring of 1946, life in the free Netherlands had seemingly gone back to normal, and the beaches in Scheveningen could once again be opened to the public. But the resort town was scarcely a shadow of the joyful, cosmopolitan destination it had been before the war. Many of the major hotels had been demolished to make room for the Atlantic Wall, and those left standing were so thoroughly run down by the German soldiers and the prisoners of war who had been detained in them postliberation, that what little was left was bulldozed by an ambitious project developer. House number 56 on the Seafront—which regained its unobstructed view of the North Sea with the demolition of the antitank wall—was one of the few buildings that survived. In that first summer after the war, the elegant residence was immediately reinstated as a guesthouse under new management, ready to welcome new guests in search of a carefree holiday by the sea.

While Dutch society was licking its wounds and trying to pick up where it left off, the Oranje Hotel was filled with Fascist prisoners. Maarten Spaans and most of the other members of the Jodenploeg were immediately detained in May 1945. They didn't deny that they had worked as bounty hunters, but they claimed to know nothing of any cruelty or abuse. "We never witnessed anyone being hit. Our bosses didn't tolerate that." Spaans experienced firsthand what it was like to be turned over to violent interrogators. He was knocked around the interrogation room like a human punching bag for hours, and in official reports he declared over and over again—sincerely or not—that he was sorry:

> I deeply regret what happened. We didn't know the
> consequences. During my service, I was always led by
> the conviction that I, as a policeman, must enforce the
> laws established by the occupying power, which there-
> fore included the German regulations against the Jews.

> Much of my bad behavior can be explained by youth-
> ful recklessness and folly.[105]

His trial was held in 1948. Spaans was convicted of complicity in 362 arrests as well as the murder of a Jewish person in hiding who had tried to flee. Initially it seemed that given his leading role and—in the words of the prosecutor—"abominable diligence," he wouldn't be able to escape the death penalty, but the ill-treatment he received after his arrest was considered a mitigating circumstance, and he ended up receiving life in prison. One by one, his former buddies claimed that they had no idea that extermination camps existed and that they too were deeply sorry about what had happened. Most ended up receiving approximately twenty years in prison.

Only Kees Kaptein, who was also arrested in 1945, remained entirely entrenched in his degenerate worldview. He exhibited a doggedness that, under different circumstances, could have almost been considered heroic. In his eyes, he had done everything in his power to make sure that the people who were caught helping Jews were released from prison—with their cooperation, of course. The "few" times he had allowed himself to go so far as to use physical violence were in situations where it was simply in the prisoner's best interest. Even the "Jews who were gassed" could only blame themselves, because "the Jewish attitude was such that it was simply impossible to have respect for them." He claimed that the dozens of reports of blackmail, abuse, rape, and extortion that had been filed against him during the war were nothing but attempts to ruin him and labeled the countless witnesses, both men and women, who had spoken out against him since the liberation "whores" and "too cowardly to be [men]."[106] On April 6, 1948, in what his counselor called a "room full of hate," Kees Kaptein was sentenced to death. About one year later, his short, criminal life was put to an end. He was one of the last of the forty-four Dutch war criminals to be executed by the Dutch state.

Neither Rika's children nor Kees Chardon's parents knew that their loved ones' bully had been executed, just as they were unaware of the trial against him and the other Jew hunters. Even though most of the victims hadn't lived to tell their stories, the evidence against their perpetrators was so overwhelming that no great effort was made to find witnesses, and even some of the people who had spoken out against them weren't called to testify. The Nods and Chardon cases weren't investigated, and no one was charged. The silence that had been so essential during the occupation seemed to have outlived the war.

Therefore, there was never any clarity about the exact circumstances surrounding their arrests. However, there was no doubt in anyone's mind that the residents of the Pijnboomstraat had been betrayed, if only for the fact that lists containing personal information about those in hiding had most definitely been seen by multiple people. Dobbe Franken was certain they had been betrayed by a Jewish Resistance fighter in her younger sister's social circle. In a futile attempt to save his own skin, he had probably given the Nazis entire lists of names as they beat him in the interrogation room. The Chardon family assumed their betrayer had been Jewish, but unbeknownst to them, the raid on the Spoorsingel was the result of a slip of the tongue by a young deserter with too little imagination to realize the impact of his words. Meanwhile, Waldy was absolutely convinced that Gerard van Haringen had betrayed them on the Pijnboomstraat. When he heard that Van Haringen had survived the war and was living on one of the West Frisian Islands, he swore off the Dutch archipelago for the rest of his life. As for Van Haringen, he was entirely unaware of the consequences of his actions. He had no idea what had happened to the Nods family and assumed that the person to blame for their arrest was a Jewish woman from Schiebroek whom he had once seen at the house on the Pijnboomstraat; in his opinion, she had come into a suspicious amount of money after the war.

The SD report of the Chardon raid simply stated that it was carried out on January 18, 1944, in response to a phone call from the Rotterdam secret police. Spaans and his colleagues confirmed this during interrogation, but the person who had tipped them off remained unnamed. In the end, the Pijnboomstraat traitor disappeared into the annals of history. The survivors lived on, each with their own suspicions, each with a hole in their heart. And they kept quiet, as Albert Helman described in his epitaph for victims of Nazi terror:

> Silently the people have dispersed: the dead lying
> in a heap—
> And I, I so often think: they haven't passed away,
> those unnamed souls, each one was a name,
> a fate, a hope, a spark of the future.[107]

In assessing what happened in the Netherlands under Nazi occupation, later generations were quick to draw hard lines between good and evil, but they hadn't experienced the war and all its ambiguity firsthand, and it was all too easy to see things as black or white. But those who had lived through it knew better: only the dead were blameless. All survivors had something to feel guilty about—if only the mere fact that they were still alive while so many others, some of whom had surely been better, braver, more deserving than they, were not.

***

Waldy, who had once posed so candidly for his father's camera as a boy, never appeared that way in photos again. Later photos of him reveal something bewildered, almost ashamed, in his eyes. That safe island that he and his parents had created in the middle of a skeptical, sometimes hostile world was gone, and their "Sonny Boy" had become a cuckoo in the nest, a situation in need of a solution. He was, in short, a problem, an unwanted package that was passed around from one person to the next.

Though his grandparents tried to be sweet to him, they had no idea what to do with their mixed-race grandson whom they had taken in mostly out of guilt. For Grandpa Van der Lans, the news of his rebellious oldest daughter's death had taken its toll on his health, and he barely survived a heart attack. His wife processed her sorrow and remorse with such Catholic devotion that her living room started to look more like a parish hall. When Waldy's aunt Hilda and uncle Jo settled in Amsterdam in 1946 and announced that they were prepared to take in their orphaned nephew, the Van der Lanses promptly took them up on their offer. Perhaps, when it came down to it, the boy would be better off with his own kind, they thought.

At first, Waldy was relieved that he would be leaving his grandparents' stuffy, incense-infused house for the laid-back atmosphere of his father's family. In Amsterdam's Surinamese-Indian community, the small-minded, bourgeois mentality of people from The Hague was even somewhat frowned upon. He got nice new clothes, they danced and went out, and he no longer had to go to church every morning. But Hilda and Jo, who had never had any children of their own, found raising their nephew to be more difficult than they had imagined. So much had changed since they had stayed on the Seafront in the shadow of the looming war. Waldy was no longer the chatty, charming moksi-moksi little boy that he had been back then, but rather a lanky young man with hunched shoulders and a skittish look in his eyes. "He has gotten so quiet," his Surinamese aunts said to each other, shaking their heads.

Around his eighteenth birthday, Waldy encountered the extremely nationalistic West Indian and East Indian student community, where he discovered ideologies that promised justice for all and no more war. He became politically aware and rebellious, and decided to quit school, though he had already fallen hopelessly behind anyway. Meanwhile, his aunt Hilda, who had left the Japanese POW camps badly bruised, was having trouble untangling the threads between the past and present. She became convinced that there were people around her who were out to get her and had charged her doorknobs with electricity. She suspected Waldy of giving them signs from behind the window. He did his best to navigate his aunt's paranoia, but it got increasingly worse, and eventually he no longer dared to invite people over for fear that his aunt might become aggressive.

Waldy had scarcely any contact with his family in The Hague anymore. Most of them still felt uncomfortable about the whole situation, especially since they had judged Rika and Waldemar so mercilessly before the war. No one wanted to be reminded of the drama, and on top of that, they were busy putting the pieces of their own lives back together after five years under occupation. And so, they all assumed that someone else would take care of Rika and Waldemar's only son; and in the end, no one did. Bertha was the only one who faithfully sent letters and invitations to Amsterdam. For her, her mother's death—which came just as she had escaped her father's dictatorial rule—had been a disastrous end to a far from tranquil youth. As she got older, she developed into the spitting image of Rika, both inside and out, and even though she had a young family of her own by then, she did what she could to hold the family together and to make sure Waldy was included.

Waldy's brothers, on the other hand, seemed content to simply forget their younger half brother, who had always been such a thorn in the family's side. The oldest, Wim, devoted his life to his family, patients, and two brothers, whom he cared for like the father he wished he'd had himself. He never spoke a word of his mother or the little brother he had never met. Only once, when his own children were nearly adults did he tell them "the story," one time and one time only: their Grandma Jans wasn't really their grandmother, their real grandmother had abandoned her family a long time ago and later passed away. The topic was then closed for further discussion. It wasn't until much later that Wim agreed to meet Waldy, and in the months before his death, he started talking about the mother he had so rigorously cut out of his life as a young boy. Only then did he confess what had held him back all those years: his sorrow over an irreversible decision and the fear of his own failure as a son.

Meanwhile, Waldy wandered through life in search of something to hold on to that he never completely found. Thanks to a chance encounter with a teacher, he picked up his studies again, and in 1951, at the age of twenty-two, he earned his high school diploma. He found a job as a trainee journalist at *Het Parool*, a Resistance-era newspaper that thrived after liberation, and started studying political science. He married a girl from a Socialist-Idealist family whom he had gotten pregnant. Neither his studies nor his marriage lasted long, but more than anything, he felt relief that he could finally leave the house of his aunt, who by then had sunk even deeper into her delusions. In one of her final moments of clarity, Hilda arranged for Waldy's last name—which was still officially Van der Lans—to be changed to that of his father and grandfather.

Koos Nods was heard from one last time. In a stiff letter to his daughter, he demanded that his grandson be sent to Venezuela, a country rife with opportunity and plenty of gold to be panned. This letter was one of the things that compelled Hilda to let Waldy marry so young. Shortly afterward, the old gold digger disappeared without a trace into the immense wilderness of central Brazil. Rumor has it that after finding a giant gemstone, he was murdered by a fellow fortune seeker. If the rumor is true, Koos died just as he had wanted to live— filthy rich.

***

The past grabbed Waldy by the throat at the age of fifty. He had just returned from Suriname, where he had immigrated with his second family in 1962, in search of his father's paradise and to get away from the Cold War hanging over Europe. But it turned out that he couldn't escape the course of world history there either, for just a few months after his arrival, the Cuban missile crisis broke out, and Suriname, too, fell under the threat of a third world war.

The psychiatrists didn't find it particularly difficult to trace the source of chronic stress in Waldy's life, and they recommended that he confront his sorrow. Following their advice, he decided to travel in his parents' footsteps. He skipped Ravensbrück—his uncles had been there in 1946 and came home more confused than they'd been before. What he didn't know was that the spot on the Schwedtsee where his mother's ashes were thrown had since been designated as what the French so aptly call *un lieu de mémoire*—a place of remembrance. Every year to this day, Dutch schoolchildren scatter flowers over the water, so in a way, Rika does get the roses she always wanted on her grave. At the Baltic Sea, Waldy found a simple memorial next to a parking lot at the beach in Neustadt. It had been placed there on May 7, 1945, at the site of a mass grave containing the remains of several victims whose bodies had washed ashore. On the stacked stones was a plaque that read: "In eternal remembrance of the prisoners of Camp Neuengamme. They lost their lives in the sinking of the *Cap Arcona* on May 3, 1945." Around the memorial were happy German families enjoying a picnic.

When it turned out that the trip hadn't really helped, the psychiatrists suggested that Waldy try putting his parents' story on paper. He was, after all, a writer by trade, and perhaps it would help him find closure. Their suggestion, however, drove him even deeper into a corner, because, in fact, he had been trying to write down his memories of his parents from the moment he had heard they weren't coming back. He had attempted to write about them in every way he knew: as a factual account ("I spent my early childhood in Scheveningen"); as a novel with his alter ego, Wam Strand, as the main character ("'I am going to write a book in German,' Wam thought, and then those rotten krauts can read for themselves how much I hate them"), and as a letter to his parents:

Strange how you two have become strangers to me. I
don't remember what you look like. The image I have
of you in photos seems outdated, as if the two of you
would no longer fit in nowadays. I know the photos
only capture a moment and you would have evolved
with the times. Maybe the two of you didn't want that.
Maybe the misery you experienced was so depressing
that what you wanted didn't even matter anymore.

I've recently been to Germany for the first time
myself. Can you blame me? Everyone is going, everyone should go at least once. I met a student my age
who was sent to the Eastern front when he was 16
years old. The Russians captured him and forced him
to spend five years of his Führer-contaminated youth
doing hard labor in Siberia. He too . . .

I am studying philosophy. Would you two have
liked that? Would you have been proud?[108]

But no matter how many hours Waldy spent behind the typewriter
and how many crumpled pieces of papers were tossed into the waste-
basket, he kept finding himself in a rut. And for as little as he had cried
when he heard the news about his parents, he now found himself shed-
ding helpless tears. For everything else he had always been able to find
words, but he wasn't able to bring his parents back to life. Every time
he tried, the story would come to a screeching halt at the same point,
at the same image: his father on the eve of the liberation standing at the
railing of the mythical floating sea palace doomed to become his fate.

THE SEA, 1945

The order came from the headquarters of the Second Tactical Air Force in Süchteln. Rumors had been flying around for weeks that Nazi bigwigs were trying to escape via the Baltic Sea to Norway and would continue the fight from there. On May 1, military intelligence announced that there were German ships fully loaded with troops in the Bay of Lübeck. When the news arrived, however, the support of British armored divisions conquering Hamburg was still the main priority. But once the port city was brought under complete Allied control on May 3, Order 7—to "destroy concentrations of enemy ships in the marine area to the west of Poel Island"—was carried out by various RAF squadrons.

At approximately eleven o'clock in the morning, eight Hawker Typhoons took off from the former Luftwaffe airbase Ahlhorn. They were among the newest and most advanced fighter-bombers, each with eight missiles under its wings that could be shot off in a salvo or aimed and fired one by one. Within a few minutes, a few dozen planes joined them from other bases, including Tempest fighters and a pair of smaller aircraft to cover the fighter-bombers. At around 11:35 a.m., the small air fleet arrived in Lübeck. In the meantime, however, a thick layer of cloud had formed over the Baltic Sea, and since the pilots had no idea what was lying below, they decided to turn back. On the way, they shelled a few military transports on the way from Schleswig-Holstein—shooting, as one of the pilots would later recall, at anything that moved.

At around two o'clock in the afternoon, they received word that the sun had broken through over the Baltic Sea. For the second time, the planes flew over the smoldering ruins of northern Germany, and within a few minutes, they had their target in sight. At 2:16 p.m., the sirens in the seaside town of Neustadt wailed. Fifteen minutes earlier the town's swastika flags had been lowered as a sign of unconditional surrender. On the ships off the coast, the passengers began waving white sheets at the approaching planes. In their striped jumpsuits, they shouted and cheered with joy.

But looking down at the giant ship and the many small ones around it, the pilots saw nothing but enemy targets floating on the shiny surface of the Baltic. It was their third mission of the day, and they had already been dropping their deadly loads on German cities night after night for months. Their chances of survival had been next to nothing, especially in the beginning—they lost on average one out of three planes per operation—and they were living on amphetamines, alcohol, and bravado. They thought nothing of the citizens they had to bomb, let alone of the Nazi scum cornered like rats down below. This would be their last operation of the war, and as always, they were automatically focused on one thing and one thing only: carrying out their mission and getting out of there as quickly as possible.

The attack started at two thirty in the afternoon. From a height of over eleven thousand feet, the bombers dived down one after the other, each one releasing its missiles in a salvo. Giant fireballs rolled across the *Cap Arcona* and the nearby vessels; the sound was deafening. The white flags of surrender vanished behind the clouds of smoke and towering splashes and were no longer visible to the smaller bombers and fighter jets handling the precision work. They rained their bombs down on any vessel that hadn't been hit yet and wiped the decks clean with their machine guns. Ten destructive minutes later, the RAF planes pointed their noses back toward their home base and flew off, disappearing above the storm suddenly gathering in the sky.

That night, one of the pilots wrote in his combat diary that the "Big Shipping Strike" was "nothing short of brilliant": "Given the circumstances, it's safe to say that a lot of Jerries found the Baltic Sea very cold today."[109] That evening, the following news arrived from the English front:

> Bombers and fighter jets carried out a massive and successful attack against concentrations of German troops on their way from Schleswig-Holstein on ships trying to reach Denmark from Kiel, Flensburg and other ports. Approximately 250 to 300 ships were attacked, including a convoy of more than fifty units. At the end of the day, the waters around Kiel, Flensburg and Lübeck were littered with burning ships.

Waldemar's world ended in chaos and flames. As the sound of the planes faded away on the horizon, the bay that had been so peaceful that morning was transformed into a deadly inferno. The vessels were left adrift, burning like torches, and in the water around them were the bodies of the dead and drowning. A nearby freighter had been hit midship and was sinking. As it went down, there was one final bang: the sound of its captain putting a bullet in his head. The *Cap Arcona* was burning from three points. The roaring fire ate its way through the walls, the carpets, the wood paneling, and the deck of the once-so-handsome ship. The Russian prisoners who had lorded over the camps were now trapped like rats belowdecks. Locked in the cargo hold in the forecabin, they had no chance of survival. Their dying screams and cries for help were overpowered by the sound of shattering glass from the dining hall, where the SS ammunition supplies were firing off into the glass ceiling one after another.

Thousands of people scurried around the ship like terrified ants. The prisoners who had been put in the cabins were struggling to make it up to the decks, meanwhile SS guards were firing shots in the stairwells, confiscating life vests, and shooting their way to the few lifeboats that hadn't yet gone up in flames. Furniture was tossed overboard for the drowning people below to grab hold of, but many of them were crushed by it. Crowded onto the few decks that were not yet ablaze, the survivors were forced to choose between the flames of hell or the icy waters below. They searched the horizon in the hope that help was on the way. But help never came, for the few minesweepers that had attempted to leave the Lübeck harbor to rescue the drowning came instantly under fire from the Allied tanks outside the city.

Approximately thirty minutes after the attack, the *Cap Arcona* began to capsize. Hundreds of passengers fell like ragdolls from her scorching hot flanks and were sucked down with the moribund ship. The seawater was breathtakingly cold—barely five or six degrees above freezing. There were even ice floes floating on the surface of the water, remnants of a winter that had been so severe that even the salty Baltic had nearly frozen solid. Many of the drowned were so exhausted and undernourished that they only survived a few minutes in the icy sea. The survivors fought with each other to secure tabletops and life vests, and from the lifeboats, the SS guards continued shooting at the people in the water. A few prisoners chose revenge over their slim chances of making it out alive. They overturned the lifeboats and strangled their former tyrants with their bare hands, ultimately going down with them.

Waldemar, the swimmer, was one of those who chose the water. He took off his shirt and lowered himself down with ropes. He hadn't swum in years, but as soon as his body hit the water, he found his rhythm. Finally, he was free. With long strokes, his arms and legs— quickly losing all feeling—cleaved their way through the water, away from the burning, smoldering ship and the terrible cries of those trapped inside it. The sun had disappeared by then, and it had started to rain;

the icy drops lashed against his face. But the sea was calm, as the Baltic usually is, and the longer he swam, the calmer it became around him. Here and there were the heads of other swimmers headed for the white dunes along the horizon, roughly two and a half miles away. And even here, dead bodies floated on the surface of the water, but these had peaceful, almost blissful, looks on their faces. As horrible as the throes of death had been for those left behind on the ship, the end had been merciful for the ones in the water, who, as the hypothermia set in, were gently swept away by the waves.

At around four o'clock in the afternoon, a regiment of tanks from the British Ninety-Eighth Field Artillery rode into Lübeck and took over the city without a struggle. A scout eyeing the horizon could have sworn he saw a gigantic, red-hot fireplace grate emerging from the sea, but he quickly realized what it was: the carcass of a ship. A few hours later, a small rescue operation would manage to save just five hundred of the eighty-five hundred prisoners from the water and the keel of the still-burning *Cap Arcona*—many of whom would die in the days to come. The event would go down in history as one of the greatest maritime tragedies of all time; it is also one of the most unknown.

At around five o'clock, Waldemar reached the beach between Pelzerhaken and Neustadt. It was low tide, and he felt solid ground beneath his feet a few hundred yards before the shore. Together with another man from the ship, he waded through the final stretch to the dry land, one foot in front of the other, numb and exhausted. Suddenly, the spitfire of machine guns rattled from the dunes. Waldemar's fellow swimmer quickly dropped down and played dead, but in that split second, he saw the black man beside him get shot and disappear under the water.

And so, Waldemar Nods died on the shores of the Baltic Sea, on May 3, 1945, at approximately five o'clock in the afternoon, barely forty-eight hours before the official end of the war. He was shot dead by soldiers in poorly fitting uniforms, their frightened boys' eyes peering out under helmets too large for their heads. Surely, they were not much older than his own son, Waldy, but they'd been raised in the glory and doctrine of their invincible Führer. They didn't know what to do, so they fired. As his blood drained into the icy water, Waldemar no longer felt any cold or pain. He was rocked by waves, all filth and misery cleansed by the sea. The water was his friend, just as it had always been.

At that moment, midday was approaching in Paramaribo. The calls of kiskadees could still be heard in the trees, but the vendors down at the Waterfront had already started packing up their wares, and shutters were being closed against the looming midday heat. The river's warm, muddy waters sloshed languidly against the docks, and Waldemar swam. He swam home.

AFTERWORD

A Sort of Happy End

I first heard the story of Rika van der Lans and Waldemar Nods while standing around the coffee machine in the editorial offices of the magazine where I worked. The couple's life story was told to me by a new colleague in the design department. Rika and Waldemar's only child, Waldy, was her father-in-law. "He is so frustrated by the fact that he has never been able to write his parents' story himself," she said. "He would be thrilled if you would do it."

Although I didn't do anything with the story at the time—my editor in chief would have never given me the time and space to write an article about two totally unknown people—I couldn't get it out of my mind. It was as if the story was still wandering around, tugging at my sleeve because it so desperately wanted to be told.

Perhaps my fascination stemmed from the fact that I was working as a journalist specializing in the reconstruction of crime stories at the time, and I was constantly confronted with the same fundamental question: on what grounds and under what circumstances do people make the wrong choice? Rika and Waldemar's bittersweet love story was a natural counterpart to my work. How, I wondered, could two people who already had so much against them—their difference in skin color, difference in age, the economic depression of the 1930s, discrimination, and the consequences of a traumatic divorce—find it in their hearts to risk their lives for other persecuted people? In other words, what inspires someone to do something good?

I guess you could say that this story became my own little investigation into the how and why of heroism based on the fates of two ordinary people who found themselves caught up in the great wheels of world history. Rika and Waldemar's lives touch two of the darkest, most taboo chapters of Dutch history, namely the slave trade and the persecution of Jewish people. However essentially different these two episodes were—the motivations of the former were primarily economic and those of the latter were ideological—they had one thing in common: racial and ethnic discrimination.

When, years later, I still couldn't shake the couple's story and finally met Waldy in person, I discovered another motivation for my desire to tell their story: the need to bring his parents back to life, if only on paper. Naturally, I realized that people disappear under the ruins of history every day, never to be found again. But still, it felt good to at least try to pull these two people out of the rubble. At the very least, it might offer some comfort to their son, who had last seen them as a fourteen-year-old boy in a prison in The Hague, and who, in his seventies when I met him, seemed to be suffering more from their loss by the day.

The first few times I visited Waldy to talk about his parents, he choked up with tears within five minutes. As his dog tried to console him, he silently handed me one of the photo albums he had managed to rescue from his parents' house. It was as if he wanted to say, "Here, look. Look how happy the three of us were together." Rarely had I ever met anyone who so thoroughly embodied the adjective "broken."

My research took me to The Hague, to Suriname, to Germany, and every time I came home, I would update him on my progress. After a while, I started to notice a change. Waldy cried less and even seemed to be enjoying the project. When he called one day to tell me that he had found in the attic the long-lost letters his parents had sent him from the concentration camps, he sounded almost triumphant. When I presented him with the first copy of the book on his seventy-fifth birthday—despite all his previous refusals to give a speech—he stood up before an absolutely silent audience and said: "Annejet, with this book, you have given me back my parents."

Those words were the best review I have received and ever will receive.

In the period that followed, something extraordinary happened. The book about two unknown figures, which no one had had any commercial expectations for, started to gradually take on a life of its own. After a modest start, *Sonny Boy*, as the Dutch edition was titled after Waldy's nickname, climbed its way up the bestseller list. And once it was there, it stubbornly held its place—first for months, and eventually for years.

Sonny Boy had become the kind of book that people recommended to each other: "You've got to read this." It has become a book that, even now, fifteen years after it was first published, is still one of the top three most popular titles in Dutch high schools. It has been translated, endlessly reprinted, and was eventually even made into a film, which later served as the Dutch submission to the Oscars for the Best Foreign Language Film.

And no one, not even I, found as much joy in the book's success as Waldy. Again and again he shared his story with the press, and each time he did, he seemed a little less broken and a little more confident. At the film premiere of *Sonny Boy*, he proudly accepted a standing ovation from the one thousand people in the audience. And later, he walked like a celebrity through the streets of Paramaribo with the film's director and accepted everyone's congratulations on the story of his father, the Surinamese Resistance hero.

Waldy, who had spent much of his adult life feeling like a cast-off, unwanted orphan, transformed into a Dutch-Surinamese prince, loved and cherished by everyone around him, just as he'd been as a little boy at home with his parents on the Seafront. And when he died a happy man in May 2012, all the Netherlands knew the story of Sonny Boy. His death was reported in every newspaper, and photos of him and his parents appeared on front pages around the country. As one of his sons put it at his widely attended funeral, his life had, despite everything, finally come to a happy end.

This story, which had started out as a conversation around the coffee machine, ended up being life changing for me as well. For starters, it convinced me that writing was my calling in life. But more than that, it taught me that although you cannot rewrite history, no matter how badly you might want to, you can give it a twist. And sometimes, such as in this case, you can even create a lot of good.

For a long time, it seemed that evil had triumphed in Waldy's life. But in the end, it was no match for the power of his story.

ACKNOWLEDGMENTS

I write books about both famous and nonfamous people, and each type comes with its own particular challenges. With the famous, you are often hindered as a biographer and researcher by the myths that people, sometimes the person in question, construct about their lives. Whereas with the nonfamous, you're faced with the tremendous disadvantage that, unlike public figures, ordinary people tend to leave behind fewer traces. This is even more the case when your subjects disappeared without a trace sixty years prior to the start of your investigation—as with Rika van der Lans and Waldemar Nods.

At first, there seemed to be no surviving evidence of these two forgotten lives other than a couple of lines in the *Weinreb Report*, a few letters, and two photo albums filled with piles of yellowing, mostly undated photographs. At that time, I even toyed with the idea of telling their story in the form of a historical novel. But as I dug deeper into the main characters and more and more material surfaced, I realized that fiction, at least in this case, is simply no match for real life.

Given that I simply could not *not* tell this story, I wrote it based on the memories of those involved and information found in archives, and in doing so, I became fully guilty of what a Dutch critic once beautifully and aptly described as "plundering the fiction writer's toolbox." However, this doesn't take away from the fact that the book is founded on authentic material and verifiable facts confirmed by the various people involved. The sources of all quotations can be found in the Sources section, along with a list of archives consulted and an abridged bibliography.

Like every reconstruction, this book was a puzzle, and it wouldn't have been possible without all the people who helped me look for the pieces. There were too many of them to name here, but a few people simply cannot go unmentioned. For starters, there was, of course, Waldy Nods; his wife, Christine Nods-de Vries; and their children, Carina Frenken-Nods and Remko Nods. Without their enthusiasm and trust, this book would have never been possible. I also couldn't have done it without the support of Rika's youngest son from her first marriage, Henk, and her grandchildren, Haaije Jansen (Bertha's son—Bertha had passed away), and Nynke Lopez Cardozo and Isabel Greydanus (Wim's daughters). Unfortunately, Rika's second son, Jan, found the past too painful to revisit and decided not to participate in the project. Out of sensitivity to his feelings, his family's last name has been changed in the text.

Then there were the many nephews, nieces, cousins, friends, and other eyewitnesses who were happy to share their memories of Waldemar and Rika, namely, Anneke Swart-Renckens, Marcel van der Lans, Jan Rolandus Hagendoorn, Pie Springvloed, Juanita Treurniet, Georgette Treurniet, Henny Radelaar-Millar, Maggee Leckie-Millar, Tini Hewitt-Hennink, and—in Paramaribo—Muriel SamSin Hewitt and Christien van Russel. Also, the two survivors of the Pijnboomstraat raid, Dobbe Kirsh-Franken and Gerard van Haringen, were willing to tell their stories.

Though the form I chose for this story compelled me to leave scholars and experts out of the book as much as possible, that doesn't mean I didn't make liberal use of their knowledge and advice. In my quests through The Hague and Scheveningen, I was led by Dr. Bart van der Boom, Harold Jansen, Danny Verbaan, Aad Wagenaar, and Boris de Munnick. I traced the Nodses' footsteps in the Dutch Resistance and the German concentration camps with the help of Dr. Hermann Kaienburg, Professor Andries van Dantzig, Margaretha de Bruijn-Chardon, Gisela Wieberdink-Söhnlein, Mies Wijnen, Leo van der Tas, and Bert and Lenie Intrès.

Then there were the heavily abused—by me, that is—employees of the various archives where I searched for clues about my main characters, people such as David Barnouw, Hubert Berkhout from the NIOD, Regina Grütter and Henri Giersthove from the Dutch Red Cross, Sierk Plantinga from the CABR Archive, Maikel Darson from the Bisschopshuis, Michael Kromodomtjo from the Centraal Bureau voor Burgerzaken, and Ernie Esajas from the Landsarchief—the latter three all located in Paramaribo. Professor André Loor, Dr. Jerry Egger, Heinrich Helstone, Laddy van Putten, Alphons Levens, Philip Dikland, Willy Oosterlen, Leonoor Wagenaar, the Vereniging Ons Suriname, and Pieter Bol from the Stichting Surinaamse Genealogie helped me navigate Suriname's history. Also, special thanks to Carl Haarnack, owner of an excellent collection of books about the history of the former colony, which he lent me with great generosity.

The advice of Frans Bubberman, former director of Bosbouw van Suriname and one of the few people who had personally visited the colony Waldemar's family had come from, as well as that of H. R. van Ommeren, descendant of Willem van Ommeren, was essential for describing the history of the Dageraad plantation as accurately as possible. (Initially, this early Surinamese history was included in the book's manuscript, but I later cut it because it wasn't considered relevant to the main plot.)

In the end, it was Cees de Kom, son of black Resistance hero Anton de Kom, who, without even realizing it, gave me the key to the story's final mystery. He and his sister had been in contact with Waldemar's fellow swimmer in the Baltic Sea, who had shared his story with them under the assumption that the man swimming beside him had been their father. However, Anton de Kom had died about a week before in the Sandbostel subcamp. In the Neuengamme Concentration Camp Memorial Archives, it was confirmed that there was only one Surinamese man aboard the *Cap Arcona*, and that was Waldemar Nods.

Captain Robert Grabowski and the crew of his *Marfret Normandie* piloted me safely across the ocean and through tropical storm Anna, and the team at Nijgh & Van Ditmar publishers accompanied me with great dedication through the peaks and valleys of the sometimes-turbulent creation process. I'm also very grateful to Em. Quer, Uitgeverij for the lovely jubilee edition published in honor of the book's twenty-fifth printing, in which—in addition to all kinds of new photos—"The Dageraad" was included as a separate story.

Equally important were my own helpers, especially Jo Simons and Piroska Nijhof. They accompanied me in my travels, shared in my experiences, and helped me make sense of it all. They tolerated the fact that putting together the pieces of someone else's puzzle often interfered with both my life and theirs, and above all, they were there to laugh in my face whenever I swore in all seriousness to never lose myself in a story again. But the one person to whom I owe the most gratitude for this book is Waldy's daughter-in-law, Sefanja Nods-Muts, who first told me the story. She did everything in her power to make this book a reality, and through it all maintained a rock-solid faith in the realization of this project.

ARCHIVES AND INSTITUTES CONSULTED

Archiv Dokumentenhaus Neuengamme, Hamburg, Germany

Camp Vught National Monument, Netherlands

Centraal archief voor Bijzondere Rechtspleging, The Hague, Netherlands

Centraal Bureau voor Burgerzaken, Paramaribo, Suriname

Diocese of Suriname, Bisschopshuis Archive, Paramaribo, Suriname

Hendrik School Archives, Paramaribo, Suriname

Jewish Historical Museum, Amsterdam, Netherlands

Landsarchief Suriname, Paramaribo, Suriname

Municipal Register, The Hague, Netherlands

National Archives, The Hague, Netherlands

National Library of the Netherlands, The Hague, Netherlands

Nederlands Instituut voor Oorlogsdocumentatie, Amsterdam, Netherlands

Oorlogsgravenstichting, The Hague, Netherlands

Royal Netherlands Institute of Southeast Asian and Caribbean Studies, Leiden, Netherlands

Royal Tropical Institute, Amsterdam, Netherlands

Stichting 1940–1945, Amsterdam, Netherlands

Stichting Oorlogs- en verzetsmateriaal, Groningen, Netherlands

Stichting voor Surinaamse Genealogie, Leiden, Netherlands

Stichting Vriendenkring Neuengamme, Buren, Netherlands

Surinaams Museum, Paramaribo, Suriname

Vrij in Suriname, Manumissieregister Database (see Vrij in Suriname, Volkstelling Burgerlijke Stand Database 1921)

SOURCES

Most of the quotations used in the text were found in various personal archives. For the sake of readability, the spelling and grammar have been adapted according to contemporary language standards.

1. Al Jolson, B. G. de Silva, Lew Brown, and Ray Henderson, "Sonny Boy," from *The Singing Fool*, 1928.
2. Sebastian Haffner, *Defying Hitler: A Memoir*, trans. Oliver Pretzel (New York: Picador, 2002), 7. Originally published in 1937.
3. Prayer card for Lambertina van der Lans. Private archive W. Nods.
4. H. W. J. van der Lans, "In Memory of My First Holy Communion. To My Dear Parents." 7 May 1903. Private archive W. Nods.
5. H. W. J. van der Lans, "In Memory of."
6. N. Govers, Een Halve eeuw in Suriname 1866–1916 ('s-Hertogenbosch, Neth.: C. N. Teulings, 1916).
7. Jacques Samuels, Schetsen en typen uit Suriname (Paramaribo, Suriname: St. Rafael Boekhandel, 1944).
8. Govers, Een Halve.
9. Bertha Hagenaar's diaries, 1930–1940. Private archive H. J. Jansen.
10. Jolson et al., "Sonny Boy."
11. Hagenaar's diaries.
12. Hagenaar's diaries.
13. H. W. J. van der Lans to her son Henk, letters, 1940–1943. Private archive W. Nods.
14. H. W. J. van der Lans to her daughter, Bertha, letters, 1931–1942. Private archive H. J. Jansen.
15. H. W. J. van der Lans to her daughter, Bertha.
16. Guest book, 1933–1942, Pension Walda. Private archive W. Nods.

17. Guest book, Pension Walda.

18. H. W. J. van der Lans to her daughter, Bertha.

19. H. W. J. van der Lans to her daughter, Bertha.

20. Hagenaar's diaries.

21. Hagenaar's diaries.

22. Hagenaar's diaries.

23. Hagenaar's diaries.

24. H. W. J. van der Lans to Mr. and Mrs. J. van der Lans, letter, 13 June 1933. Private archive W. Nods.

25. Guest book, Pension Walda.

26. H. W. J. van der Lans to Mr. and Mrs. J. van der Lans.

27. Guest book, Pension Walda.

28. Walda Pension brochure. Private archive W. Nods.

29. H. W. J. van der Lans to her daughter, Bertha.

30. H. W. J. van der Lans to Mr. and Mrs. J. van der Lans.

31. Hagenaar's diaries.

32. Hagenaar's diaries.

33. Hagenaar's diaries.

34. Hagenaar's diaries.

35. Hagenaar's diaries.

36. Hagenaar's diaries.

37. Hagenaar's diaries.

38. H. W. J. van der Lans to her daughter, Bertha.

39. Albert Helman, Zuid-Zuid-West (Utrecht, Neth.: De Gemeenschap, 1926).

40. Guest book, Pension Walda.

41. Hagenaar's diaries.

42. Hagenaar's diaries.

43. H. W. J. van der Lans to her daughter, Bertha.

44. H. W. J. van der Lans to her son Henk.

45. Hagenaar's diaries.

46. Guest book, Pension Walda.

47. Guest book, Pension Walda.

48. H. W. J. van der Lans to her son Henk.

49. H. W. J. van der Lans to her son Henk.

50. H. W. J. van der Lans to her son Henk.

51. H. W. J. van der Lans to her daughter, Bertha.

52. H. W. J. van der Lans to her daughter, Bertha.

53. J. W. G. van der Lans to M. van der Lans, letters, 1941–1942. Private archive M. van der Lans Jr.

54. H. W. J. van der Lans to M. van der Lans, letter, 1943. Private archive M. van der Lans Jr.

55. H. W. J. van der Lans to M. van der Lans.

56. J. W. G. van der Lans to M. van der Lans.

57. H. W. J. van der Lans to M. van der Lans.

58. J. W. G. van der Lans to M. van der Lans.

59. Guest book, Pension Walda.

60. H. W. J. van der Lans to her daughter, Bertha.

61. H. W. J. van der Lans to M. van der Lans.

62. *Kees Chardon 31 August 1919–April 1945*. Private records of the Chardon family, Municipal Archive of The Hague.

63. *Chardon 31 August 1919–April 1945*.

64. Guest book, Pension Walda.

65. H. W. J. van der Lans to M. van der Lans.

66. M. Spaans, Procès-verbal 18 January 1944, and interrogation report 1946. CABR-dossier.

67. Spaans, Procès-verbal and interrogation report.

68. Spaans, Procès-verbal and interrogation report.

69. Paula Chardon, Een beschrijving van 13 dagen gevangenisleven in de Polizei-Gevangenis in Scheveningen. 1944. Archive Jewish Historical Museum.

70. Chardon, Een beschrijving.

71. Chardon, Een beschrijving.

72. Chardon, Een beschrijving.

73. Chardon, Een beschrijving.

74. Chardon, Een beschrijving.

75. K. Kaptein interviews. CABR Archive.

76. K. Kaptein interviews.

77. W. H. Nods to J. van der Lans, letters, 5 March 1944–1945. Private archive W. Nods.

78. Chardon, Een beschrijving.

79. Chardon, Een beschrijving.

80. *Chardon 31 August 1919–April 1945*.

81. *Chardon 31 August 1919–April 1945*.

82. W. H. Nods to J. van der Lans.

83. *Chardon 31 August 1919–April 1945*.

84. W. H. Nods to J. van der Lans.
85. H. W. J. van der Lans to J. van der Lans, letters, 1944. Private archive W. Nods.
86. W. H. Nods to J. van der Lans.
87. W. H. Nods to J. van der Lans.
88. H. W. J. van der Lans to J. van der Lans.
89. H. W. J. van der Lans to J. van der Lans.
90. H. W. J. van der Lans to J. van der Lans.
91. H. W. J. van der Lans to J. van der Lans.
92. W. H. Nods to J. van der Lans.
93. D. de Montagne to H. W. J. van der Lans, letter, 9 December 1944. Private archive W. Nods.
94. W. H. Nods to J. van der Lans.
95. Chardon, Een beschrijving.
96. *Chardon 31 August 1919–April 1945.*
97. *Chardon 31 August 1919–April 1945.*
98. Red Cross Archive, The Hague, file number 33438, H. W. J. van der Lans.
99. Red Cross Archive, file number 33438.
100. J. van der Lans to W. Nods, letter, 14 July 1945. Private archive W. Nods.
101. M. van der Lans to J. W. G. van der Lans, letters, 1941–1942. Private archive M. van der Lans Jr.
102. W. Nods, personal memoirs and diaries, 1944–1955. Private archive W. Nods.
103. Prayer card for Hendrika Nods-van der Lans. Private archive W. Nods.
104. Telegram from Jo Herdigein and Hilda Nods. Private archive of W. Nods.
105. Spaans, Procès-verbal and interrogation report.
106. K. Kaptein interviews.
107. N. Slob [pseudonym of Albert Helman/Lodewijk "Lou" Lichtveld], "Niemand sprak; geen kreet, geen kreunen," in De Diepzeeduiker, 1945.
108. Nods, personal memoirs and diaries.
109. Gunther Schwaberg, "Angriffsziel Cap Arcona," in Stern 4 (March 2003): 3, 10, 17, 24, 30.

ABRIDGED BIBLIOGRAPHY

Anton de Kom-Abraham Behr Institute. *A. de Kom, zijn strijd en ideeën*. Amsterdam, Neth.: Sranan Buku, 1989.

Bal, C. *Scheveningen-Den Haag 1940–1954 / Van Dorpen Stad tot Stützpunktgruppe Scheveningen*. The Hague, Neth.: The Hague Municipality, 1996.

Bartelink, E. J. *Hoe de tijden veranderen, het relaas van een lange "plantage-carrière."* Paramaribo, Suriname: H. van Ommeren, 1916.

Benjamin, H. D., and Joh. Snelleman. *Encyclopaedie van Nederlandsch West-Indië*. The Hague/Leiden, Neth.: Nijhoff and Brill, 1914–1917.

Benoit, Pierre Jacques, Silvia W. de Groot, and Chris Schriks. *Reis door Suriname: beschrijving van de Nederlandse bezittingen in Guyana*. Zutphen, Neth.: Walburg Pers, 1980.

Berg, Max vanden. "Zuid-Holland 1940–1945, een jonge provincie, de oudste geschiedenis." *Contactblad '40–'45* (2003): 9–16.

Boekhoven, G., and P. Lanink. *Memoires Neuengamme*. Haren, Neth.: 1980.

Bolwerk, P. B. M. *Paramaribo in oude ansichten.* Zaltbommel, Neth.:
   Europese Bibliotheek, 2000.

Boom, Bart van der. *Den Haag in de Tweede Wereldoorlog.* The Hague,
   Neth.: Uitgeverij Lakerveld, 1995.

Bruijning, C. F. A., and W. Gordijn. *Encyclopedie van
   Suriname.* Edited by J. Voorhoeve, Amsterdam-Brussel:
   Uitgeversmaatschappij Argus Elsevier, 1977.

Chardon, Paula. *Een beschrijving van 13 dagen gevangenisleven in
   de Polizei-Gefängnis te Scheveningen.* 1944. Jewish Historical
   Museum Archive.

De Vraagbaak—Almanak voor Suriname 1925, 1928. (Continuation of
   Surinaamsche almanak). Paramaribo: 1925, 1928.

Doerry, Martin. *Mijn gewonde hart. Het leven van Lilli Jahn, 1900–
   1944.* Amsterdam, Neth.: De Bezige Bij, 2003.

Emmer, P. "Slavernij-debat is aan herziening toe." *de Volkskrant,* 26
   June 2004.

Emmer, P. C. *De Nederlandse slavenhandel 1500–1850.* Amsterdam,
   Neth.: Uitgeverij De Arbeiderspers, 2000.

Gerding, Pearl I. *Op weg naar grotere hoogten, de geschiedenis van een
   kerk.* Paramaribo, Suriname: Evangelisch Lutherse Kerk, 2002.

Giltay Veth, D., and A. J. van der Leeuw. *Het Weinreb-rapport.* The
   Hague, Neth.: Staatsuitgeverij, 1976.

Haarnack, Carl. Publication of speech in Lodewijk "Lou" Lichtveld exhibition books. Amsterdam, Neth.: Koninklijk Instituut voor de Tropen, 8 November 2003.

Helman, Albert. *Avonturen aan de wilde kust.* Alphen aan den Rijn: Sijthoff, 1982.

Helman, Albert. *De foltering van Eldorado, een ecologische geschiedenis van de vijf Guyana's.* 's-Gravenhage, Neth.: Uitgeverij Nijgh & Van Ditmar, 1983.

Helman, Albert. *De stille plantage.* Uitgeverij Conserve, Schoorl 1997. First published 1931 by Nijgh & Van Ditmar ('s-Gravenhage, Neth.).

Helman, Albert. *Zuid-Zuid-West.* Utrecht, Neth.: De Gemeenschap, 1926.

Het Grote Gebod—Gedenkboek van het verzet in LO en LKP (2 vols). Kampen, Neth.: Uitgeverij J.H. Kok, 1951.

Hijlaard, Marius Th. C. *Zij en ik.* Paramaribo, Suriname: 1978.

Hove, Okke ten, and Frank Dragtenstein. "Manumissies in Suriname 1832–1863." *Bronnen voor de Studie van Afro-Surinaamse samenlevingen* 14 (1997).

"In memoriam Cornelis Chardon." *De Zwerver, weekblad van de stichting LO-LKP,* 22 June 1946.

Janssen, René. *Historisch-geografisch Woordenboek van Suriname naar A.J.van der Aa, 1839–1851.* Utrecht, Neth.: Vakgroep Culturele Antropologie, 1993.

Jong, L. de. *Het Koninkrijk der Nederlanden in de Tweede Wereldoorlog.* 14 vols. The Hague, Neth.: Staatsuitgeverij, 1969–1991.

Kaienburg, Hermann. *Das Konzentrationslager Neuengamme 1938–1945.* Bonn, Ger.: Verlag J. H. W. Dietz Nachfoler, 1997.

Kees Chardon 31 August 1919–April 1945. Private records of the Chardon family, The Hague Municipal Archives, no date.

Klein, P. W., and Justus van der Kamp. *Het Philips Kommando in kamp Vught.* Amsterdam, Neth.: Contact, 2004.

Kom, A. de. *Wij slaven van Suriname.* Amsterdam, Neth.: Het Wereldvenster, 1990.

Korver, H. J. *Varen op de West.* Bussum, Neth.: De Boer, 1975.

Leuwsha, Tessa. *Reishandboek Suriname.* Rijswijk, Neth.: Uitgeverij Elmar B.V., 2002.

McLeod, Cynthia. *Herinneringen aan Mariënburg.* Paramaribo, Suriname: VACO Uitgeversmaatschappij Paramaribo, 1998.

Munnick, B. de. *Uitverkoren in uitzondering? Het verhaal van de Joodse'Barneveld-groep' 1942–1945.* Amsterdam, Neth.: Schaffelaarreeks nr. 24, 1992.

Neus-van der Putten, Hilde. *Susanna du Plessis, portret van een slaven-meesteres.* Amsterdam, Neth.: KIT Publishers, 2003.

Nods, C. "Vijftig jaar geleden ging Lily Nods naar het 'Verre Rio.'" *Weekkrant Suriname,* 7 April 1984.

Olink, Hans. "De nodeloze ondergang van de Cap Arcona." *de Volkskrant,* 30 May 1987.

Oostindie, Gert, and Emy Maduro. *In het land van de overheerser. Antillianen en Surinamers in Nederland 1634/1667–1954.* Essays from the Royal Netherlands Institute of Southeast Asian and Caribbean Studies. Dordrecht, Neth.: Foris, 1986.

Rolsma, H. *Neuengamme. De ramp in de bocht van Lübeck.* In possession of the Stichting Oorlogs- en Verzetsmateriaal Groningen, Groningen, no date.

Samuels, Jacques. *Schetsen en typen uit Suriname.* Paramaribo, Suriname: St. Rafael Boekhandel, 1944. First published 1904.

Schön, Heinz. *Ostsee '45.* Stuttgart, Ger.: Motorbuch, 1998.

Schwaberg, Gunther. "Angriffsziel Cap Arcona." *Stern* 4 (March 2003): 3, 10, 17, 24, 30.

Slob, N. [pseud. Albert Helman]. "Niemand sprak; geen kreet, geen kreunen." *De Diepzeeduiker,* 1945.

Stipriaan, A. van. *Surinaams contrast.* Leiden, Neth.: KITLV Uitgeverij, 1993.

Stuldreher, Coenraad J. F. "Das Konzentrationslager Herzogenbusch–ein 'Musterbetrieb der SS'?" In: *Die Nationalsozialistischen Konzentrationslager–Entwicklung und Struktur.* Herausgegeben von Ulrich Herbert, Karin Orth und Christoph Dieckmann. Göttingen, Ger.: Wallstein Verlag, 1998. Band i, p. 327–349.

Surinaamsche (staatkundige) Almanak, Almanak voor de Nederlandsche West-Indische bezittingen. The Hague, Neth.: 1792–1846 (with gaps).

Verbaan, Danny. *Verlaten vesting, de evacuatie van Scheveningen in 1942/'43.* Museum Scheveningen, Historical Series, no. 11, Rijswijk, Neth.: Uitgeverij Elmar B.V., 2003.

"Verkeerde medische behandeling? Een doodelijk malarie-geval aan boord van het s.s. 'Oranje Nassau.' Aangifte van een Deensche familie." *De Telegraaf* (15 November 1927).

Vernooij, J. G. *De Rooms Katholieke kerk in Suriname vanaf 1866.* Paramaribo, Suriname: Westfort, 1974.

Vink, Steven. *Suriname door het oog van Julius Muller, fotografie 1882–1902.* Amsterdam, Neth.: KIT/SSM, 1998.

Weber, E. P. *Gedenkboek van het 'Oranjehotel': celmuren spreken, gevangenen getuigen, onze gevallen verzetshelden.* Amsterdam, Neth.: Nelissen, 1947.

ABOUT THE AUTHOR

Annejet van der Zijl is one of the best-known and most widely read literary nonfiction writers in the Netherlands. In addition to other works, she has written biographies of Dutch children's author Annie M. G. Schmidt; Prince Bernhard, the husband of former Dutch queen Juliana; and Gerard Heineken, the founder of the famous beer empire. Her nonfiction has been awarded the M. J. Brusse Prize for the best work of journalism and has been nominated for the Golden Owl and the AKO Literature Prize. She is the author of *An American Princess*, which spent more than fifteen weeks at the top of the national bestseller list in the Netherlands and was short-listed for the Libris History Prize. In 2012, she was awarded the Golden Quill for her entire oeuvre.

ABOUT THE TRANSLATOR

Kristen Gehrman is from Charleston, South Carolina, and studied linguistics and literary translation at the University of Lausanne in Switzerland. She now lives in The Hague, where in addition to her work as a literary translator, she teaches academic writing and translation. While translating *The Boy Between Worlds*, she enjoyed biking around The Hague and Scheveningen and visiting the places where Rika and Waldemar had been.